Debra Murray's
Flip Pan™
REVOLUTION

Acknowledgments

I am so thrilled with the success of our *Cook's Companion Flip Pans*™! Curtis Anderson you are a genius!

Thank you Mark Linduski for helping Curt design these, and all your wonderful support for the past 3 years. You are a true angel for me!

I must thank my beautiful daughter Nevar, you are not only beautiful, smart, and fun, you are my best friend! Thanks for always encouraging me! I have the best Mom, dad, sister and bonus Mom, Myrna. Thanks for all your love and support!

I am so grateful for our Fabulous group on Facebook, The Flip Pan™ Group. To date we have over 6000 members and growing. It delights me daily to see your posts and how you all constantly encourage each other. I could not keep up if it were not for my dear friend Josephine Cook. I adore all my friends on Facebook, you make me feel so loved and your encouragement and support of my shows means the world to me. I adore waking up in the morning and seeing all the gorgeous food you are making in your various Flip Pans™!

I so need to thank my best friend Laurie Bain. Not only has she stood by me for over 30 years for some of the best and worst days of my life; but, Laurie diligently helped me select, test, write, and edit this book. I would have never made my deadlines without her! Thanks for being the best friend anyone could hope for! Laurie is also an awesome food stylist!

Chris Davis my photographer—you just keep getting better every day in every way! Thank you for your gift and your faith, I am a better person every time I am around you!

Thank you to Erin Hauswald for bringing the Flip Pans™ to life as my stylist on Evine Live. Thank you to Michele Trombley, my book designer. Thank you to Shannon Kelly, my website designer and assistant. Thank you to Penny Markowitz-Moses for editing.

Josephine Cook

Contents

Tips for Success with Flip Pans™

The Flip Pan™ Revolution! To date we have 8 different models of Flip Pans™ of various sizes and colors. With close to 200,000 sold, these brilliant designs are on their way to revolutionizing how people cook.

The Flip Pans™, when closed, are sealed with a rubber gasket and held together by two magnets which prevents steam from escaping. This will retain 90 percent of the cooking steam which turns the pan into a low pressure-pressure cooker. This means you will retain more flavor and more nutrients than cooking with other pans. You will also experience faster cooking times. In this book I have included 100 different recipes with some for each of the different Flip Pans™.

What is low pressure cooking? Approximately 3 PSI. This is when the cooking liquid or the moisture from the food you are cooking creates steam. By prohibiting the escape of the steam, it reduces cooking time over a conventional covered pot—water boils at a higher temperature under pressure, thus speeding up the cooking process. Plus, bathing food in steam seals in flavor and nutrients that are typically boiled out on the stove top. So with the Flip Pans™, you get better tasting, juicier, meals faster!

The first thing I always recommend, and the manufacturer will as well, is clean your Flip Pan™ with soap and water, towel dry, then I rub or season the ceramic surface with olive oil. The ceramic is a fabulous, chemical-free nonstick, but it is water based. Like any water-based product, occasional seasoning of the surface will give your surface a longer life. To have optimum release, I recommend using a healthier nonstick such as avocado, coconut or grape seed oil, all readily available at the grocery store. In the grocery stores, there are tremendous new products like pump, not aerosol, nonstick sprays which are healthy—like grape seed and coconut oils. Most of my recipes will call for preheating without oil or spray, top and bottom. But, I am a person who will never leave that pan unattended. If you find you are a person who may leave the pan in the preheat stage, I recommend adding oil to the pan, so the nonstick does not turn brown. I heat my pan until I feel the heat coming off the pan, then I add my spray or my oil.

I know we call the Flip Pan™, a Flip Pan™; but that does not mean everything needs to be flipped. Do not flip if adding cooking liquid. Because of the steam hole, this will create a mess on your stove, and the added weight could cause the pan to open while turning.

My favorite technique is to brown the protein on both sides, flipping if using the Versa Flip Pan™, then I add my liquids such as stock or wine. As for the UniVersa Flip Pan™, I only flip when making kettle corn. The Proaster you would never flip. But because of the locking mechanism and the gasket, you will steam roast, which will produce the most moist delicious roasts of your life.

How to get the best results cooking proteins: Typically I keep the Flip Pan™ closed for most dishes, except steak, tuna or scallops. The first thing I do when cooking any protein is to make sure the poultry, steak, pork, fish or seafood is very dry, with all residual moisture removed. I let my proteins sit at room temperature for at least 20 minutes. Then I rub the proteins with just enough oil to adhere the seasonings I will put on them. Then, I make sure the pan is hot. I love to begin with a couple minute sear per side on medium high, then I back the temperature to medium. As I mentioned before, for steak, tuna and scallops, I will cook the entire piece 90% before closing the lid for the last minute or two to infuse with a cooking liquid. The other meats I like to preheat the Flip Pans™ top and bottom, then cook. For example, I cook a chicken breast for 5 minutes per side.

A very important point when cooking eggs in a Flip Pan™ is that the ceramic nonstick coating performs better at 225 degrees on the induction burner, and low on all other cook tops. When you cook on a higher temperature than that, ceramic can seize. So remember wipe or spray your pan with oil, let preheat on low or 225. Let the eggs set up for a minute before trying to move, and you will have perfect eggs not swimming in oil using this technique. I try to use an induction burner for eggs for this reason. It's a very effective way to maintain the perfect temperature.

When making sandwiches or French toast, always preheat your pan top and bottom, then add the sandwiches. If the pan is really hot you can turn the burner down low. This will prevent burning and keep the sandwich from getting soggy. You could otherwise cook with the Flip Pan™ open, turning with tongs, then closing at the last minute to melt the cheese or heat the center.

We do not encourage baking above 300 degrees in the oven, except for the Proaster. Some of you may have ovens that are not calibrated, and heating the pans too hot in the oven can cause the magnets to fall out. You can easily bake on top of the stove with your Flip Pans™. Just preheat top and bottom, then cook low and slow, and you will have perfect cakes in under 30 minutes.

How do I calculate how long to cook the meat? This is not an exact science, but I have found that if I preheat the pan top and bottom, and because of the seal of low pressure the pan creates closed, I take all typical cook times and cut in half. If a recipe calls for pork chops to cook 10 minutes per side for ½ inch pork chops, I would cook them for 5 minutes per side. Every now and again, I wish I had cooked them a bit less, or I need to give them a few minutes longer. But 90% of the time that is the perfect calculation.

I am including a chart in this book that will give you a basic time line, and say whether or not to use liquid. I calculate you should add 1 tablespoon of cooking liquid for every minute an item is cooking, unless I have noted not to add liquid at all.

Most recipes in this book call for a higher temperature than the cooking chart indicates. The cooking chart is designed to keep your pan pristine, but to achieve the desired results of the recipe, I used the temperature best suited for that.

I am so happy you have purchased our fabulous pan and I hope it will bring you as much joy using it as it does me and my wonderful friends in the Flip Pan™ Group on Facebook. I have asked some of my most loyal recipe posters to contribute to this Flip Pan™ book.

Happy Flipping!!

Much Love,

Debra Murray

Cooking Chart for Flip Pans™

Here is a basic cooking guideline for proteins, vegetables, pasta, and rice. I did not include sandwiches, as these would depend on thickness and would not follow a chart. There are sandwich recipes in this book you could use as a guideline.

If you are using the Versa Flip Pan™ you would flip the pan. If using the UniVersa Flip Pan™ you would open the pan, flip the food, then re-seal. Please note, PS on the chart below means per side.

FOOD	THICKNESS/WEIGHT	COOK TEMP	COOK TIME	LIQUID	TEMP
STEAK	1 –1 ½ Inch	Low/Medium	3–4 Min Per Side	No	Med Rare
PORK CHOPS	1–1/12 Inch	Medium	10 Min PS	Yes	Well
CHICKEN	1–11/2 Inch	Low/Medium	5 Min PS	Choose	Well
BURGERS	1–1 ½ Inch	Low/Medium	4-5 Min PS	No	Med/Well
SAUSAGES	1 Pound	Low/Medium	5 Min PS	Yes	Well
SALMON	1 Pound	Low/Medium	3 Minutes	No	Well
FISH FILETS	1 Pound	Low/Medium	2 Min PS	Yes	Well
BACON	6 Strips	Medium	3 Min PS	No	Med
SHRIMP	1 Pound	Medium	3 Min PS	Choose	Med/Well
EGGS	2 Large	Medium	2 Min PS	No	Runny
HAM STEAK	1 Inch	Low/Medium	3 Min PS	No	Well
DRUMSTICKS	1 Pound	Low/Medium	7 Min PS	Choose	Well
CHICKEN THIGHS	1 Pound	Low/Medium	8 Min PS	Choose	Well
SPATCHCOCK	3 Pound	Low/Medium	12 Min PS	Choose	Well
BB RIBS	½ Slab	Low/Medium	15 Min PS	Yes	Well
SPARE RIBS	6 Ribs	Low/Medium	20 Min PS	Yes	Well
POT ROAST	3 Pounds	Medium	3 Hours	Yes	Well
PORK ROAST	3 Pounds	Medium	2 ½ Hours	Yes	Well
CORNED BEEF	3 Pounds	Medium	4 Hours	Yes	Well
POTATOES	2 Pounds	Low/Medium	20 Minutes	Yes	Tender
ZUCCHINI	1 Pound	Low/Medium	3 Min PS	No	Done
ONIONS	1 Pound	Low/Medium	4 Min PS	No	Tender
ASPARAGUS	1 Pound	Low/Medium	2 Min PS	Yes	Tender
CORN	4 Ears	Low/Medium	4 Min PS	Yes	Tender
ARTICHOKES	2 Halved	Low/Medium	10 Min PS	Yes	Tender
GREEN BEANS	1 Pound	Low/Medium	9 Minutes	Yes	Tender
BROCCOLI	1 Pound	Low/Medium	4 Minutes	Yes	Tender
BRUSSELS SPROUTS	1 Pound	Low/Medium	10 Minutes	Yes	Tender
CARROTS	6–7 Medium	Low/Medium	7 Minutes	Yes	Tender
EGGPLANT	1 Medium	Low/Medium	5 Min PS	No	Tender
KALE	1 Pound	Low/Medium	8 Minutes	Yes	Tender
MUSHROOMS	1 Pound	Low/Medium	4 Min PS	Yes	Tender
PEPPERS	2 Medium	Low/Medium	3 Min PS	No	Tender
WINTER SQUASH	2 Pounds	Low/Medium	12 Minutes	Yes	Tender
PASTA	2 Cups Dry/4 Cups Boiling Liquid	Low/Medium	8–10 Minutes	Yes	Al Dente
RICE (WHITE)	2 Cups Dry/3 Cups Boiling Liquid	Medium	15 Minutes	Yes	Fluffy
QUINOA	2 Cups Dry/2 Cups Boiling Liquid	Medium	12 Minutes	Yes	Fluffy

Balsamic Pan Seared Pork Chops

Serves 4

INGREDIENTS

4 pork chops, center cut, bone in

¼ teaspoon sea salt

¼ teaspoon freshly ground pepper

1 teaspoon rosemary, chopped

¼ cup balsamic vinegar

1 tablespoon extra-virgin olive oil

1 tablespoon butter

DIRECTIONS

1. Preheat Flip Pan™ on each side over medium heat for 2–3 minutes per side. Season pork chops with salt and pepper.

2. Add oil, butter and rosemary and heat. Add pork chops to Flip Pan™ and close lid. Cook for 7 minutes, flip the pan, and cook for an additional 7 minutes.

3. Open lid remove the pork chops to a platter and deglaze pan with vinegar, pour sauce over pork chops.

4. Serve Immediately.

Braised Carrots with Balsamic Vinegar

Serves 2–4

INGREDIENTS

1 tablespoon extra-virgin olive oil

1 small onion, diced

3 cloves garlic, crushed

10 young carrots, tops trimmed and peeled

1 tablespoon balsamic vinegar

3 fresh thyme sprigs

Sea salt and freshly ground pepper to taste

DIRECTIONS

1. Preheat Flip Pan™ on each side over medium heat for 2–3 minutes per side.

2. Add oil, heat and add onion and garlic; close lid, sauté for 1–2 minutes.

3. Open lid, add remaining ingredients and continue to cook an additional 7–8 minutes, shaking occasionally until carrots are tender.

4. Serve warm.

Brussels Sprouts and Bacon with Gorgonzola Cheese

Serves 4-6

INGREDIENTS

2 tablespoons extra-virgin olive oil

4 slices of bacon diced

2 large shallots, halved lengthwise, sliced crosswise

1 pound Brussels sprouts, stem trimmed and cut lengthwise

8 ounces steamed chestnuts

½ teaspoon sea salt

¼ teaspoon freshly ground pepper

1 cup chicken stock

1/3 cup heavy cream

3 tablespoons chopped fresh chives

½ cup Gorgonzola, crumbled

DIRECTIONS

1. Preheat Flip Pan™ over medium heat for 2-3 minutes.

2. Add oil, and when heated, add bacon pieces and cook until crisp with lid closed, about 3 minutes.

3. Remove the bacon to a paper towel and add the shallots and sauté for 1 minute with lid open.

4. Add Brussels sprouts and sprinkle with salt and pepper, sauté for 1 minute.

5. Add stock, close lid, and bring to a boil.

6. Simmer until Brussels sprouts are tender, about 5-6 minutes.

7. Open lid and boil until most liquid evaporates, about 4 minutes.

8. Add cream and cook until Brussels sprouts are coated with cream, about 3 minutes.

9. Mix in chives and bacon pieces, transfer to a serving bowl, sprinkle with Gorgonzola cheese and serve.

Chicken Breasts Stuffed with Goat Cheese and Roasted Red Peppers

Serves 4

INGREDIENTS

4 boneless skinless chicken breasts, butterflied

1 (10 ounces) box frozen spinach, thawed and drained

½ cup goat cheese

Roasted red peppers

¾ teaspoon sea salt, divided

½ teaspoon freshly ground pepper

Toothpicks

Oil for spraying

1 medium onion, diced

1 cup chicken stock

2 garlic cloves, minced

2 teaspoons dried thyme

1 teaspoon red pepper flakes

¼ cup parsley, chopped

DIRECTIONS

1. In a medium sized bowl, mix spinach, goat cheese, ½ teaspoon sea salt and pepper until well mixed.

2. Butterfly each chicken breast by sticking the tip of a very sharp knife into the thickest part of the chicken breast cutting it almost halfway through. About a ½ inch from the end of the breast, spread the breast open like pages of a book. Place ¼ of the cheese mixture on the top of each breast, spread and top with roasted red peppers.

3. Close the chicken breasts and secure with 3 toothpicks.

4. Preheat Flip Pan™ on each side over medium for 2–3 minutes per side.

5. Spray with oil and place chicken breasts in Flip Pan™; close lid and cook for 5 minutes.

6. Flip the pan and cook for 4 minutes longer.

7. Open lid, remove chicken breasts to a platter. Add garlic, onion, red pepper flakes, ⅛ teaspoon salt, close lid and cook 2–3 minutes.

8. Add stock and leave lid open, scraping up the browned bits at the bottom of pan. Cook for several minutes to reduce liquid by half. Add dried thyme.

9. Pour sauce over chicken breasts, sprinkle with parsley and serve.

Chicken Thighs with White Beans

Serves 4

INGREDIENTS

2 tablespoons extra-virgin olive oil

4 (1 pound) skin-on, boneless thighs

¾ teaspoon kosher sea salt, divided

¼ teaspoon freshly ground pepper

1 cup finely chopped red onion

1 (15 ounces) can cannellini beans, undrained

2 cloves garlic, minced

⅓ cup pesto (see recipe)

DIRECTIONS

1. Preheat Flip Pan™ on each side over high heat for 2–3 minutes per side.

2. Oil the chicken thighs and season with salt and pepper and add to the Flip Pan™ skin side down.

3. Cook for 2 minutes, reduce heat to medium-high, and cook an additional 5 minutes or until skin is crispy.

4. Flip pan and cook an additional 2 minutes or until done. Remove to a platter and cover to keep warm.

5. Return Flip Pan™ to high heat, add onion, garlic and pepper to the pan and sauté for 2 minutes or until tender.

6. Add beans to the pan, cook 1 minute and stir in remaining salt. Gently stir in pesto.

D'Ann Matthews' Apricot Chicken

Serves 2–4

INGREDIENTS

1 ½ pounds chicken tenders

1 tablespoon butter

1 tablespoon extra-virgin olive oil

1 cup assorted red, green and yellow bell peppers, cut into small chunks

½ cup onion, cut into small chunks

Pepper to taste

1 clove garlic, minced

1 can (15 ounce) apricot halves in syrup

3 tablespoons soy sauce

2 tablespoons brown sugar

1 tablespoon crystallized ginger, finely chopped

DIRECTIONS

1. Preheat Flip Pan™s on each side over medium heat for 3–4 minutes.

2. Add butter and olive oil, and heat over medium heat for 3–4 minutes.

3. In a bowl add apricots with juice, garlic, soy sauce, brown sugar and ginger.

4. Stir until everything is blended.

5. When butter and oil are heated add bell pepper and onions to the Flip Pan™, let them sweat for a few minutes.

6. Add chicken and season with pepper, cook until browned, about 5 minutes on each side.

7. Stir in apricot mixture, turn pieces to coat and bring to a boil.

8. Close lid and reduce heat to medium; set timer for 35–40 minutes.

9. D'Ann likes to serve this with rice.

Easy Mu Shu Pork

Serves 4

INGREDIENTS

1 tablespoon peanut oil

12 ounces boneless pork, thinly sliced strips

3 cups mushrooms, sliced

½ cup green onion, bias cut

4 cups cabbage, shredded

2 garlic cloves, minced

2 tablespoon soy sauce

1 teaspoon sesame oil

¼ teaspoon crushed red pepper

8 flour tortillas, 7–8 inch

¼ cup hoisin sauce

DIRECTIONS

1. Preheat Flip Pan™ on each side over medium heat; add oil and heat.

2. Add meat and cook 2–3 minutes while stirring. Remove to a plate.

3. Add mushrooms and garlic and cook over medium heat for 2–3 minutes.

4. Add cabbage, close lid and cook for 1 minute.

5. Return pork to Flip Pan™ add soy sauce, sesame oil and red pepper; close lid and cook for an additional 1–2 minutes, or until heated through.

6. Serve on warm tortillas topped with hoisin sauce and sprinkled with green onion.

Green Beans with Tomatoes and Onions

Serves 2-4

INGREDIENTS

Nonstick spray

4 cup fresh green beans, trimmed and cut in half

1 medium onion, sliced

2 cups cherry or grape tomatoes, washed and cut in half lengthwise

½ cup fresh basil, cut in ribbons

Sea salt and freshly ground pepper to taste

DIRECTIONS

1. Preheat Flip Pan™ on each side over medium heat for 2-3 minutes per side.

2. Spray inside of Flip Pan™, top and bottom, add green beans and onions and close lid.

3. Cook over medium heat for 3-4 minutes shaking occasionally, Flip pan and continue to cook for an additional 3-4 minutes shaking occasionally.

4. Open lid and add tomatoes, salt, pepper and basil, close lid and cook for 1 minute more.

5. Serve warm.

Halibut with Tomatoes, Capers and Olives

Serves 4

INGREDIENTS

4 halibut filets

¼ teaspoon sea salt

¼ teaspoon freshly ground pepper

4 tablespoons extra-virgin olive oil, divided

2 large shallots, chopped

¼ teaspoons crushed red pepper flakes

4 plum tomatoes, seeded and chopped

½ Kalamata olives, pitted and chopped

½ cup basil

1 tablespoon small capers, drained

⅓ cup bottled clam juice

⅛ teaspoon lemon zest

DIRECTIONS

1. Preheat Flip Pan™ on each side over medium heat for 2–3 minutes per side.

2. Over medium heat, 2 tablespoons of oil.

3. Season fish filets with salt and pepper.

4. When oil is hot add fish, close lid, cook for 2 minutes, Flip pan and cook another 2 minutes or until fish is just opaque in center.

5. Transfer fish to a platter and cover.

6. Heat remaining oil in Flip Pan™, add shallots and red pepper, sauté 1 minute.

7. Add remaining ingredients, except basil, close lid and cook for about 3 minutes or until sauce is slightly thickened.

8. Stir in basil, season with salt and pepper to taste.

9. Spoon sauce over fish and serve.

Osso Buco

Serves 4-6

INGREDIENTS

2 pounds meaty veal shanks

1 tablespoon extra-virgin olive oil

½ cup onions, diced

½ cup celery, diced

½ parsnips, diced

2 garlic cloves, minced

1 teaspoon kosher sea salt

½ teaspoon freshly ground pepper

½ cup sweet vermouth

1 can (4 ½ ounces) petite diced tomatoes

1 sprig thyme

1 teaspoon orange zest

1 ½ cup beef stock

DIRECTIONS

1. Preheat Flip Pan™ on both sides over medium heat for 2-3 minutes per side.

2. Season veal shanks with salt and pepper on both sides.

3. Add the oil to the Flip Pan™ and heat for two minutes. Add the veal to the Flip Pan™ and cook for 3 minutes per side. Add the remaining ingredients, close lid.

4. Cook over medium low heat for 45 minutes.

5. Transfer veal to a platter and reduce sauce.

6. Using a blender, puree sauce.

7. Pour sauce over veal and serve.

Peaches and Cream Stuffed French Toast

Serves 4

INGREDIENTS

1 cup brown sugar

1 ½ cups cream

1 tablespoon vanilla extract

4 large eggs

½ teaspoon ground cinnamon

1 can (29 ounces) sliced peaches, drained

2 ounces peach liqueur

1 package (8 ounces) cream cheese

8 slices day-old French bread, cut into 1-inch slices

Oil for spraying

Powdered sugar for dusting

DIRECTIONS

1. In a shallow baking dish, mix eggs, cream, cinnamon, vanilla and sugar.

2. In a separate bowl, blend peaches peach liqueur, cream cheese.

3. One at a time, dip 4 slices of bread into the egg mixture, top each slice with peach mixture; remove to a platter.

4. Dip remaining slices of bread in remaining egg mixture, placing each slice on the top of the others to form 4 sandwiches.

5. Preheat Flip Pan™ on each side over medium heat for 2–3 minutes per side; spray with oil.

6. Place each sandwich on the griddle side; close lid.

7. Cook for 4 minutes, flip pan and cook for an additional 3 minutes or until golden brown and cooked through.

8. Dust with powdered sugar and serve immediately.

Sautéed Chicken with Saffron-Tomato Vinaigrette

Serves 4

INGREDIENTS

3 tablespoons white balsamic vinegar

1 ½ teaspoons hot paprika

⅛ teaspoon saffron threads, crumbled

⅛ teaspoon red pepper flakes

4 tablespoons extra-virgin olive oil, divided

½ cup shallots, minced

2 tablespoons fresh thyme, divided

2 ½ cups heirloom cherry tomatoes, halved

4 skinless, boneless chicken breasts

½ teaspoon sea salt

¼ teaspoon freshly ground pepper

1 head curly endive, torn in pieces

DIRECTIONS

1. In a bowl, mix together vinegar, ½ teaspoon paprika, red pepper flakes and saffron. Add 3 tablespoons oil, shallots and 1 tablespoon thyme.

2. Stir in tomatoes and season to taste with salt and pepper.

3. Preheat Flip Pan™ on each side over medium heat for 2-3 minutes per side.

4. Heat remaining oil; Sprinkle chicken breasts with 1 teaspoon remaining paprika, 1 teaspoon of thyme and salt and pepper.

5. Add chicken breasts to Flip Pan™, close lid and cook until cooked through over medium heat, flipping frequently, cook for 10-12 minutes. Transfer chicken breasts to a cutting board and slice.

6. Divide endive between 4 plates and top each with one sliced chicken breast.

7. Drizzle vinaigrette over each.

Steak au Poivre

Serves 4

INGREDIENTS

4 Tenderloin steaks, 6–8 ounces each, 1 ½-inches thick

2 ounces extra-virgin olive oil

Kosher sea salt

2 tablespoons whole peppercorns

⅓ cup Cognac, plus 1 teaspoon

1 cup heavy cream

DIRECTIONS

1. Let filets sit out for 30 minutes prior to cooking. Rub each steak with oil and season with salt.

2. Coarsely crush peppercorns in a mortar and pestle and spread on a plate evenly.

3. Press the filets on both sides into the peppercorns to coat, set aside.

4. Preheat Flip Pan™ on each side over medium heat for 2–3 minutes each side.

5. Place filets in Flip Pan™, griddle side down raise heat to medium high, cook with lid open for 4 minutes, turn each steak and cook for an additional 2–3 minutes, depending or desired doneness.

6. Remove filets to a serving platter and cover. Off the heat, add Cognac to the pan and carefully ignite the alcohol with a long match.

7. Gently shake the pan until the flames die. Return pan to the heat and add the cream. Bring mixture to a boil and whisk until the sauce coats the back of a spoon, approximately 5–6 minutes.

8. Add teaspoon Cognac and season to taste with salt. Add filets back to pan close Flip Pan™ and cook for 2 minutes longer for medium, spoon sauce over and serve.

Sharon Huskey's Easy Parmesan Chicken Strips

Serves 4

◆

INGREDIENTS

3 boneless, skinless chicken breasts, cut into desired strips

½ cup Italian bread crumbs

3 tablespoons Parmesan, grated

Salt and pepper to taste

3 tablespoons mayonnaise

Spritz of coconut oil

DIRECTIONS

1. Mix dry ingredients in a gallon size self-sealing bag.

2. Rinse and dry chicken, spread with mayonnaise on both sides.

3. Place 3 to 5 pieces of chicken into bag and close; shake well

4. Preheat Flip Pan™ on each side over medium heat for 2–3 minutes per side.

5. Quickly spritz chicken with coconut oil and place in Flip Pan™; close lid and cook for 3–4 minutes.

6. Open lid and turn chicken pieces over, close lid and cook another 3 minutes.

7. Deliciously moist and fork cut tender. Enjoy!

Stuffed Grilled Trout with Lemons, Herbs and Onions

Serves 2-4

INGREDIENTS

2 (8 ounces) whole trout cleaned and scaled

1 tablespoon extra-virgin olive oil

1 teaspoon coarse kosher sea salt

¼ teaspoon coarsely ground pepper

2 lemons, sliced thin

1 medium onion, sliced thin

1 Roma tomato sliced thin

2 sprigs fresh dill

2 sprigs fresh thyme

¼ cup dry white wine

DIRECTIONS

1. Rinse and pat dry trout with paper towels. Rub both sides with olive oil and sprinkle with salt, pepper and set aside.

2. Stuff each trout cavity with a layer of lemons, followed by a layer of onions, tomatoes a sprig of dill and 1 sprig of thyme each.

3. Preheat Flip Pan™ on each side over medium heat for 2-3 minutes per side.

4. Add olive oil and heat. Carefully place trout in Flip Pan™ and close the lid.

5. Cook for 5 minutes, Flip pan and cook for an additional 5 minutes.

6. Open lid, add wine, close lid and cook for 5 additional minutes.

7. Garnish with remaining lemon slices and serve.

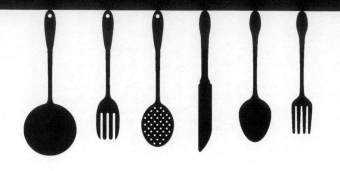

Veggie Lasagna

Serves 4

◆

INGREDIENTS

1 tablespoon olive oil

1 medium zucchini, sliced

1 med. Red pepper, seeded and chopped

1 med. Onion, chopped

½ teaspoon salt

¼ teaspoon fresh ground pepper

3 cloves garlic, chopped

1 28-ounce can crushed tomatoes

6 oz. no-boil lasagna noodles

1 cup ricotta

8 ounces' mozzarella shredded

¼ cup Parmesan cheese

¼ cup chicken or vegetable stock

Fresh basil for garnish

DIRECTIONS

1. Preheat Flip Pan™ top and bottom over medium heat for 2 minutes per side.

2. Add the oil to the Flip Pan™ and heat for 2 minutes.

3. Add the zucchini, peppers and onions and salt and pepper.

4. Close Flip Pan™ and cook for 2 minutes. Flip and add garlic and close and cook 2 minutes longer.

5. Add in the crushed tomatoes and close Flip pan and cook for 4 minutes.

6. Remove all but 1 cup of sauce to a large bowl.

7. Top sauce with 2 of the lasagna noodles, drop dollops of ricotta over the noodles and sprinkle with half the mozzarella and Parmesan.

8. Top with two more lasagna noodles and top that with more sauce to cover noodles. Repeat with the remaining noodles and cheese.

9. Top with the stock. Close Flip Pan™ and cook over medium for 15 minutes.

10. Let rest before serving. Garnish with basil leaves.

Chicken with Tomatoes and Pancetta

Serves 4–6

INGREDIENTS

6 ounces pancetta

1 whole chicken, cut into 8 pieces

1 teaspoon kosher sea salt

1 teaspoon freshly ground pepper

3 garlic cloves, sliced thinly

2 anchovy filets

¼ teaspoon red pepper flakes

1 can (28 ounces) whole tomatoes

¼ teaspoon dried thyme

½ cup fresh basil, chopped and divided

8 ounces mozzarella, cut into ¾ inch pieces

DIRECTIONS

1. Preheat UniVersa Flip Pan™ over medium heat, add pancetta and oil cook until browned.

2. Remove pancetta with slotted spoon to a paper towel.

3. Season the chicken with salt and pepper.

4. Add chicken to Flip Pan™, with lid open and sear until browned on all sides; transfer to a plate.

5. Add garlic, anchovy, pepper flakes to Flip Pan™ cover and cook for 1 minute

6. Stir in tomatoes, ½ of the basil and thyme; break up tomatoes and close lid and cook for 12 minutes.

7. Return chicken, and close the lid open cook chicken until it is cooked through, about 15 minutes.

8. Scatter mozzarella pieces over the chicken and close lid,

9. Cook about 3 minutes until cheese is melted.

10. Garnish with pancetta and the other ½ basil and serve.

Eggplant, Fennel and Sausage Ziti

Serves 4–6

INGREDIENTS

5 ounces Italian sausage, casings removed

4 cups eggplant, peeled and chopped

2 medium fennel bulbs, trimmed, cored and thinly sliced

¼ teaspoon crushed red pepper

½ tablespoon sea salt

1 tablespoon extra-virgin olive oil

1 can (14 ½ ounces) crushed fire roasted tomatoes

1 cup chicken stock

2 tablespoons tomato paste

3 cloves garlic, minced

1 teaspoon Italian seasoning

8- ounces dried ziti

½ cup fresh basil

1 cup mozzarella cheese, shredded

DIRECTIONS

1. Preheat Flip Pan™ over medium heat, add oil and heat.

2. Add eggplant and salt; close lid and cook for 5 minutes, shaking occasionally.

3. Remove eggplant to a bowl and add sausage; close lid and cook 5 minutes.

4. Add eggplant and remaining ingredients, except cheese, close lid cook on medium heat 15 minutes.

5. Open lid, sprinkle with cheese, close lid cook an additional 2–3 minutes, or until cheese is melted.

6. Serve immediately.

Georgina Budney's Buffalo Chicken Pasta

Serves 4–6

INGREDIENTS

1 lb. thin Spaghetti

1 teaspoon salt

1 ½ lb. ground chicken

3 cups chicken stock

1 cup green onions sliced

1 cup celery chopped small

1 ½ cup buffalo wings sauce

½ cup crumbled blue cheese

Versa Flip Pan™ and UniVersa Flip Pan™

DIRECTIONS

1. Place the Flip Pan™ on medium heat and brown ground chicken.

2. When chicken is cooked through and fat drained away, stir in the buffalo wings sauce.

3. Turn heat to low and simmer.

4. Add the chicken stock, onions and celery to the UniVersa Flip Pan™ and bring to a boil.

5. Stir in pasta and cook until liquid evaporates. About 6-7 minutes.

6. Stir in the chicken mixture. Mix well.

7. When serving, add crumbled blue cheese on top.

Hearty Fisherman's Stew

Serves 6–8

INGREDIENTS

4 cups fish stock or chicken stock

2 cups red bell pepper, chopped

1 ½ cups fingerling potatoes, quartered

1 cup chopped onion

1 cup chopped celery

1 can (6 ½ ounces) chopped clams, with clam juice

2 tablespoons Worcestershire marinade for chicken

1 bay leaf

1 teaspoon dried thyme

6 cloves garlic, minced

½ teaspoon kosher sea salt

¼ teaspoon freshly ground pepper

2 pounds cod, skinless and filleted

1 pound jumbo shrimp, peeled, de-veined with tails on

1 tablespoon Italian parsley, chopped

DIRECTIONS

1. Preheat Flip Pan™ over medium heat for 2–3 minutes.

2. Add all ingredients except fish and shrimp and parsley to the Flip Pan™ and bring to a boil.

3. Reduce heat to a simmer, close lid and cook about 10 minutes.

4. While cooking, rinse and pat dry fish and shrimp, cut fish into 1-inch chunks.

5. Add fish and shrimp into the stew; reduce heat and simmer for 2-3 minutes with lid closed or until fish flakes and shrimp is opaque.

6. Remove from heat, remove and discard bay leaf.

7. Sprinkle with parsley and serve.

Jacqueline's Pumpkin Soup

Serves 4–6

◆

INGREDIENTS

2 tablespoons extra-virgin olive oil

2 large onions, sliced

1 medium shallot

2 pounds fresh pumpkin, cubed

1 pound Roma tomatoes, cubed

1 medium carrot peeled and diced

4–5 threads saffron

6 cups chicken stock

2 ounces heavy cream

½ cup pumpkin seeds, toasted

3 ounces Parmesan cheese, grated

Sea salt and freshly ground pepper to taste

DIRECTIONS

1. Preheat UniVersa Flip Pan™ for 3 minutes over medium; add oil and heat.

2. Add onions and shallots, close lid and cook until tender, shaking occasionally, about 4–5 minutes.

3. Add remaining ingredients except pumpkin seeds, Parmesan cheese and heavy cream. Close lid.

4. Cook over medium-low heat for 25–30 minutes, stirring occasionally.

5. Open lid, and using an immersion blender, puree soup.

6. Ladle into bowls, swirl in cream, sprinkle with pumpkin seeds and Parmesan cheese.

Josephine Cook's Chicken Marsala

Serves 4

INGREDIENTS

1 lb. boneless, skinless, chicken breast, sliced thin, pat dry

1 lb. mushrooms, sliced

¾ cup Marsala wine

¾ cup chicken broth or stock

3 cloves garlic, chopped

3 Tbsp. butter

2 Tbsp. extra virgin olive oil

½ cup flour, divided

1 tsp. salt

1 tsp. fresh ground pepper

2 Tbsp. fresh parsley, chopped

Avocado oil, coconut oil, or olive oil spray

Warm platter

DIRECTIONS

1. Open the lid of the UniVersa Flip Pan™ (5 Qt.) and spray the inside of the lid and the bottom with avocado spray.

2. Close the lid and place on the stove. Heat griddle side, first, for 2 minutes on low heat.

3. Pat the chicken to remove moisture.

4. In a bowl, add the flour, salt and pepper (reserve 1 Tbsp. for thickening)

5. Open the lid and add the butter and oil, close the lid for a minute or so, to combine the butter and oil. Do this on low heat.

6. Dredge chicken in flour and shake the excess off.

7. Open lid of pan, sauté chicken until brown over medium heat for 4–5 minutes per side.

8. Remove to a warm platter.

9. Reduce the heat to low. Add the mushrooms and chopped garlic and sauté them for 3–4 minutes.

10. Add the Marsala wine and the chicken stock or broth, stir and close the lid.

11. Reduce the sauce for 3 minutes. Open the lid and take 3 Tbsps. of the liquid and add

12. the reserved Tbsp. of flour and mix until smooth. Add it back to the pan and stir until smooth.

13. Add the chicken to the mushrooms and sauce, spooning the sauce all over the chicken. Sprinkle the chopped parsley on top.

14. Close the lid and cook for 3 minutes.

Lamb Stew with Leeks and Artichokes Hearts

Serves 6–8

INGREDIENTS

3 ½ pounds boneless lamb shoulder, trimmed of excess fat, cut into 2-inch pieces

Course sea salt and pepper

1 ¼ cups fresh Italian parsley, chopped

3 garlic cloves, minced

1 tablespoon lemon zest

3 tablespoons extra-virgin olive oil

2 large leeks (white and pale green parts only), thinly sliced

1 large onion, thinly sliced

1 sprig fresh thyme

1 ½ cups chicken stock

3 cups frozen artichoke hearts, thawed and drained

DIRECTIONS

1. Place lamb pieces in a bowl and season with salt and pepper; cover and let stand for 30 minutes.

2. In a bowl, combine 1 cup chopped parsley, minced garlic, and lemon zest. Reserving remaining parsley to garnish.

3. Preheat Flip Pan™ over medium heat for 2–3 minutes. Add oil and heat.

4. Working in batches add lamb and cook until well browned on all sides, about 5–7 minutes per batch.

5. Transfer lamb to a bowl, add leeks and onions to Flip Pan™, cook until softened, about 5 minutes.

6. Add parsley mixture and thyme sprig and stir for 30 seconds.

7. Return lamb pieces and any accumulated juice to the Flip Pan™ and add stock bring to boil; close lid.

8. Reduce heat to simmer and cook until lamb is very tender, about 1 ½ hours.

9. Open lid, add drained artichoke hearts, close lid and simmer to heat artichokes, about 5–6 minutes.

10. Remove and discard thyme sprig. Serve immediately.

New England Style Salmon Chowder

Serves 6–8

◆

INGREDIENTS

3 pounds fresh, skinless salmon filets

1 tablespoon butter

½ cup fennel, chopped

3 cloves garlic, minced

4 cups chicken or vegetable stock

1 ½ pounds Yukon gold potatoes, cut into 1-inch cubes

½ teaspoon sea salt

¼ teaspoon freshly ground pepper

1 sprig fresh thyme

1 ½ cups half and half

2 tablespoons all-purpose flour

1 teaspoon lemon zest

DIRECTIONS

1. Pat dry salmon dry and cut into 1-inch pieces.

2. Preheat Flip Pan™ over medium heat for 2–3 minutes, when heated add butter and melt.

3. Add fennel and cook with lid open about 5 minutes, stirring occasionally.

4. Add garlic and cook an additional minute.

5. Add in the next five ingredients (through thyme), bring to a boil, reduce heat to a simmer; close lid.

6. Cook about 4–5 minutes or until potatoes are tender.

7. Remove and discard thyme sprig.

8. In a bowl combine 1 cup of the half and half and flour; stir into soup.

9. Simmer while stirring until slightly thickened; stir in salmon.

10. Close lid, cook 2–3 minutes, open lid and stir in remaining half and half until heated through; sprinkle in lemon zest.

11. Serve immediately.

Mike Caldwell's Homemade Sloppy Joes

Serves 4-6

INGREDIENTS

2 pounds ground beef

1 medium bell pepper, seeded and chopped fine

32-ounces tomato sauce

Sugar to taste

DIRECTIONS

1. Preheat UniVersa Flip Pan™ over medium heat for 2-3 minutes.

2. Add meat and cook over medium heat until browned, drain excess fat.

3. Add bell pepper and cook until softened.

4. Add as much sauce as you like and cook until simmering.

5. Add sugar to taste, (Mike likes his sweet).

6. Reduce heat to low, close lid and simmer for 30-40 minutes

7. Serve on rolls of your choice.

Texas Style Chili

Serves 6–8

INGREDIENTS

2 tablespoons extra-virgin olive oil

2 pounds ground beef sirloin

1 pound ground pork

1 red bell pepper, diced

1 medium onion, diced

3 cloves garlic, minced

2 teaspoons chili powder

2 whole chipotles in adobo sauce, chopped fine

1 teaspoon cumin

2 teaspoon sea salt

¼ teaspoon freshly ground pepper

1 cup beef stock

2 cans (14 ounces) tomatoes with green chilies and lime

2 tablespoons tomato paste

1 can (15 ounces) dark red kidney beans, drained

DIRECTIONS

1. Preheat Flip Pan™ over medium heat for 2–3 minutes per side; add oil and heat.

2. Add beef and pork and break up with a wooden spoon; close lid and cook for 5 minutes, or until cooked through, stirring occasionally.

3. Open lid, pour off excess fat and add onions, red peppers and garlic, close lid and cook for an additional 3 minutes, stirring occasionally.

4. Add remaining ingredients except beans, close lid and cook for 25–30 minutes.

5. Open lid, add beans and cook until heated through. Serve immediately

6. Garnish with cheese and sour cream!

Tomato Quinoa Soup

Serves 2–4

INGREDIENTS

1 cup white or red quinoa, rinsed and cooked

2 tablespoons butter

1 tablespoon extra-virgin olive oil

2 medium shallots, minced

2 cloves garlic, minced

1 tablespoon fennel seeds

2 cans (28 ounces each) petite diced tomatoes

2 cups chicken or vegetable broth

¼ cup roasted pine nuts

1 teaspoons basil

½ teaspoon crushed red pepper

DIRECTIONS

1. Preheat Flip Pan™ for 2–3 minutes. Add butter and oil and heat.

2. Add shallots, garlic, and fennel seeds. Close lid and cook 4–6 minutes until vegetables are tender, shaking occasionally.

3. Open lid, add tomatoes, add chicken stock or vegetable stock, close lid and increase heat to medium-high until simmering, simmer about 15 minutes, shaking occasionally.

4. Open lid and using an immersion blender, puree mixture until smooth.

5. In a small bowl, combine cooked quinoa, pine nuts, basil and red pepper.

6. Serve soup warm topped with quinoa.

Flip Around Flip Pan™

Banana Marshmallow Hazelnut Spread Quesadillas

Serves 2

INGREDIENTS

2 7-inch flour tortillas

½ tablespoon butter softened

1 tablespoon cinnamon and sugar, combined

1 banana sliced into ⅛ inch rounds

2 tablespoons marshmallow fluff

2 tablespoons hazelnut spread

Nonstick spray

DIRECTIONS

1. Spread each tortilla with butter.

2. Place cinnamon and sugar on a plate, press butter side of each tortilla into sugar mixture.

3. Place on a cutting board sugar side down and spread one tortilla with Marshmallow the other with the hazelnut spread.

4. Put the banana slices on the marshmallow, top with the hazelnut spread tortilla.

5. Preheat the Flip Around Flip Pan™ over medium heat 3 minutes per side.

6. Spray the Flip Pan™ with nonstick spray, add the quesadilla.

7. Cook for 3 minutes per side.

8. Remove to a cutting board let rest 3 minutes before cutting with a pizza cutter.

Basil Cream Chicken

Serves 4

INGREDIENTS

¼ cup milk

¼ cup dry bread crumbs

¼ teaspoon sea salt

¼ teaspoon freshly ground pepper

¼ teaspoon dried thyme

2 tablespoons butter, divided

1 tablespoon extra-virgin olive oil

4 boneless, skinless chicken breasts

½ cup chicken stock

1 cup heavy cream

1 can (4 ounces) pimentos

1 cup diced petite tomatoes

¼ cup basil ribbons

½ cup Parmesan cheese, grated

2 tablespoons cream cheese

DIRECTIONS

1. Preheat Flip Pan™ on each side over medium heat for 2–3 minutes per side; add butter and oil.

2. In a shallow bowl, combine bread crumbs, salt, pepper and thyme. Place milk in a separate shallow bowl.

3. Dip chicken in milk, dip into the bread crumb mixture, and coat well on both sides.

4. Add chicken to Flip Pan™, close lid and cook for 4–5 minutes, Flip pan and cook for additional 4–5 minutes or until cooked through and juices are clear.

5. Remove chicken to a plate and set aside. Add chicken broth to Flip Pan™ and bring to a boil over medium heat.

6. Stir in cream, pimentos, and tomatoes, bring to a boil, close lid and cook for 1 minute, stirring occasionally.

7. Open lid, reduce heat and add Parmesan, cream cheese and basil. With lid open, cook and stir until heated through.

8. Add chicken back to Flip Pan™ and spoon sauce over chicken to coat.

9. Serve immediately.

Fluffy Omelet

Serves 2

INGREDIENTS

4 large eggs, separated

1 tablespoon unsalted butter, melted

¼ teaspoon salt

¼ teaspoon cream of tartar

½ cup Parmesan cheese, grated

Nonstick spray

DIRECTIONS

1. In a small bowl, whisk together egg yolks, melted butter and salt together.

2. Place egg whites in bowl of stand mixer and sprinkle with cream of tartar over surface.

3. Fit stand mixer with whisk and whip egg whites on medium-low speed until foamy, 2-2 ½ minutes.

4. Increase speed to medium-high and whip until peaks start to form, 2-3 minutes. Fold egg yolk mixture into egg whites until blended well.

5. Preheat Flip Pan™ on each side over medium heat for 2–3 minutes per side.

6. Spray inside of Flip Pan™ on top and bottom, add egg mixture spreading into even layer; close lid

7. Shake continuously while cooking over medium high heat for 2–3 minutes, Flip pan.

8. Sprinkle Parmesan cheese evenly over the omelet, close lid and continue to cook for another 2–3 minutes depending on how wet you like your omelet.

9. Run spatula around edges of Flip Pan™ to loosen omelet, shaking gently to release.

10. Slide omelet on to platter and serve.

11. To add vegetables and/or meats, sauté in Flip Pan™ before you add egg mixture, and continue recipe as written.

Chocolate Chip Cookie

Serves 4–6

INGREDIENTS

1 cup (2-sticks) unsalted butter, softened

½ cup granulated sugar

1 cup brown sugar

1 teaspoons vanilla extract

2 large eggs

2 ¼ cups all-purpose flour

1 teaspoon baking soda

1 teaspoon salt

2 cups (12-ounce package) semi-sweet chocolate chips

DIRECTIONS

1. Preheat oven to 300 degrees.

2. In a mixing bowl, combine butter, brown sugar and granulated sugar and beat, using a hand or stand mixer, until fluffy.

3. Add vanilla, stir 30 seconds and mix in 1 egg at a time, mixing well with the addition of each egg.

4. In another bowl add flour, baking soda and salt and mix; slowly add in flour mixture to the butter, sugar mixture.

5. Stir in chocolate chips. Using the griddle side of the pan, press the dough into the bottom of the pan to form a giant cookie.

6. Place the cookie on the middle rack and bake for 25–30 minutes.

7. Cool cookie in pan on a cooling rack.

Garlic Thyme Lamb Chops

Serves 4

◆

INGREDIENTS

4 lamb chops, (6–8 ounces), trimmed of excess fat

Course sea salt and pepper to taste

2 tablespoons extra-virgin olive oil

10 ounces frozen pearl onions, thawed, drained and patted dry

5 cloves garlic, minced

3 sprigs thyme

2 tablespoons tomato paste

½ cup dry red wine

1 ½ cup chicken broth

DIRECTIONS

1. Preheat Flip Pan™ on both sides over medium heat for 2–3 minutes per side.

2. Pat dry lamb chops and season with salt and pepper; add oil and heat.

3. When oil is heated add lamb chops in single layer.

4. Close lid and cook for 2–3 minutes, Flip pan and cook for additional 2 minutes; Remove chops to a plate.

5. Add onions to the Flip Pan™, close lid and cook 2–3 minutes until brown; add thyme, garlic and tomato paste and cook about 1 minute with lid open.

6. Add wine and reduce by half, about 1 minute.

7. Stir in broth and place chops and any juices back in Flip Pan™, close lid and simmer for about 2–3 minutes, until internal temperature is 125–130 degrees for rare.

8. Serve immediately.

Greek Frittata

Serves 2–4

INGREDIENTS

8 large eggs

1 ounce half and half

Nonstick spray

1 tablespoon extra-virgin olive oil

¼ teaspoon sea salt

⅛ teaspoon red pepper flakes

4 cups fresh baby spinach

½ cup onions, chopped

2 cloves garlic, minced

½ cup mushrooms, chopped

1 cup feta cheese

DIRECTIONS

1. Preheat Flip Pan™ over medium heat 3–4 minutes each side. Spray top and bottom with nonstick spray.

2. Add oil and heat, when heated, add spinach, onions, garlic, mushrooms, red pepper flakes and salt, sauté 5 minutes.

3. In a bowl add eggs and half and half, whip gently with wire whisk.

4. Add eggs to Flip Pan™, mix gently and sprinkle feta cheese on top.

5. Close lid and cook over medium heat for 5minutes, flip and cook 3 minutes longer or until frittata is set.

6. Serve immediately.

Inside out BBQ Chicken Avocado Quesadillas

Serves 2

INGREDIENTS

2 tablespoon mayonnaise

2 flour tortillas

¼ cup grated Parmesan on a plate

¼ cup cooked chicken meat (rotisserie chicken is perfect)

2 tablespoons BBQ Sauce

1 small ripe avocado diced

½ cup Mozzarella Cheese Shredded

DIRECTIONS

1. Smear the mayonnaise on one side of each tortilla.

2. Press mayonnaise side of tortilla into the grated cheese.

3. Place one tortilla on a plate Parmesan side down.

4. Mix chicken with BBQ sauce.

5. Spread the chicken over the tortilla, top with avocado chunks, top with cheese.

6. Top with remaining tortilla Parmesan side up.

7. Preheat the Flip Around Flip Pan™ over medium heat for 3 minutes per side.

8. Slide the quesadilla into the Flip Pan™, cook for 3-4 minutes per side.

9. The outside should be crunchy the inside gooey!

Italian Sausage-Mushroom Frittata Stack

Serves 6

◆

INGREDIENTS

1 pound Italian sausage, cooked and drained, cut into ¼ -inch slices

8 large eggs

⅓ cup heavy cream

½ cup Romano cheese, divided

1 ½ teaspoons sea salt, divided

Oil for spraying

¾ cup sliced mushrooms

2 slices roasted red peppers

½ cup fresh baby spinach

1 medium onion, halved and thinly sliced

2 tablespoon fresh basil, minced

2 garlic cloves, minced

⅛ teaspoon freshly ground pepper

1 package (8 ounces) cream cheese softened and room temperature

DIRECTIONS

1. In a large bowl, whisk eggs, cream, ¼ cup Romano cheese and 1 teaspoon salt.

2. Preheat Flip Pan™ on each side over medium heat for 2–3 minutes per side.

3. Spray with oil and add mushrooms, spinach and onions; close lid and cook over medium heat until tender.

4. Open lid and add sausage, basil, garlic, pepper and remaining salt. Close lid.

5. Cook for 1 additional minute; open lid and transfer to a bowl; stir in cream cheese and remaining Romano cheese.

6. Preheat Flip Pan™ on each side over medium heat for 2–3 minutes per side, spray with oil.

7. Pour in ⅔ cup of the egg mixture, close lid and shake to distribute egg mixture around the pan; cook for 60 seconds, flip pan and cook for an additional 60 seconds.

8. Open lid and remove to a platter; cover and keep warm.

9. Repeat with remaining egg mixture.

10. Place one frittata on a serving platter and layer sausage mixture equally between layers with the last frittata on top. Cut into wedges and serve warm.

Shakshuka Eggs Basted in Spicy Tomatoes

Serves 2

INGREDIENTS

2 tablespoons extra virgin olive oil

1 small onion, diced

¼ cup roasted red pepper, diced

2 cloves garlic, minced

1 teaspoon oregano

¼ teaspoon dried thyme

¼ teaspoon turmeric

¼ teaspoon cumin

½ cup roasted red pepper

¼ teaspoon paprika

¼ teaspoon sea salt

¼ teaspoon red pepper flakes

1 can (14 ½ ounces) petite diced tomatoes

4 large eggs

DIRECTIONS

1. Preheat Flip Pan™ on each side over medium heat for 2–3 minutes per side.

2. Add oil and heat, add onions, roasted red pepper, garlic, oregano, thyme, turmeric, cumin, paprika, salt, pepper and red pepper flakes.

3. Close Flip Pan™ and cook for 2 minutes over medium.

4. Stir in tomatoes: close lid and simmer for 15 minutes.

5. Open lid and make 4 round wells in sauce and crack one egg in each well. Close lid.

6. Cook until whites are set and yolk are runny. About 1 minute.

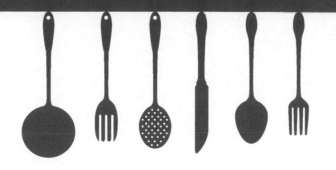

Swiss Steak

Serves 4–6

INGREDIENTS

2- pounds round steak, cut into portions

1 can (28 ounces) petite diced tomatoes

½ cup beef stock

1 large onion, sliced

½ teaspoon sea salt

¼ teaspoon freshly ground pepper

¼ teaspoon garlic powder

1 tablespoon extra-virgin olive oil

DIRECTIONS

1. Preheat Flip Pan™ on both sides over medium heat for 2–3 minutes per side.

2. Season meat on both side with salt, pepper and garlic powder.

3. Add oil and heat. Place round steak pieces into the Flip Pan™, close lid and brown for 2–3 minutes, Flip pan and brown for another 2–3 minutes. Open lid and add onions, tomatoes and beef stock; close lid.

4. Cook an additional 25 minutes, or until meat is fork tender.

5. Serve over rice.

Coq au Vin

Serves 4–6

INGREDIENTS

1 whole chicken, rinsed and cut into pieces

1 tablespoon flour

1 teaspoon sea salt

½ teaspoon freshly ground pepper

2 tablespoons butter

8 onions, peeled

1 pound whole mushrooms

2 sprigs thyme

2 cups dry red wine

1 cup chicken stock

1 teaspoon sugar

DIRECTIONS

1. Assemble Triple Flip Pan™ by attaching the griddle base pan to the grill cover and preheat over medium heat for 3–4 minutes per side.

2. Rub chicken with flour, salt and pepper.

3. Add butter to Flip Pan™ and let melt. Add chicken pieces to the Flip Pan™ and cook until golden brown.

4. Add remaining ingredients to the Flip Pan™; close lid.

5. Cook 30 minutes over medium heat.

6. Transfer chicken, mushrooms and onions to a platter, and let liquid reduce for 10 minutes.

7. Ladle sauce over the chicken and serve.

Brunch in a Skillet

Serves 4

INGREDIENTS

6 strips of bacon

6 cups frozen cubed hash brown potatoes

¾ cup red bell pepper

½ cup chopped onion

1 teaspoon sea salt

¼ teaspoon red pepper flakes

4 large eggs

½ cup cheddar cheese, shredded

DIRECTIONS

1. Assemble Triple Flip Pan™ by attaching the griddle base pan to the grill cover and preheat over medium heat for 3-4 minutes per side. Open lid and spray with oil.

2. Add bacon, close lid and cook for 3 minutes, Flip pan and cook for an additional 3 minutes or until bacon is crispy and cooked through.

3. Remove bacon to a paper towel to drain, when cool, crumble bacon and set aside. Reserving 2 tablespoons of bacon drippings.

4. Add potatoes, red pepper, onion, salt and red pepper flakes to the drippings; close lid and shake.

5. Cook for 7 minutes, Flip pan and cook an additional 7 minutes or until potatoes are browned and tender, shaking occasionally.

6. Make 4 wells in potato mixture and break an egg into each well; close lid.

7. Cook over low heat for 8-10 minutes; open lid and sprinkle with bacon and cheese.

8. Serve immediately.

Cauliflower Pizza Crust

Serves 4

INGREDIENTS

1 head of cauliflower

½ cup shredded Parmesan

½ cup shredded mozzarella

2 eggs beaten

½ teaspoon salt

¼ teaspoon garlic powder

DIRECTIONS

1. 1 head of cauliflower stems removed. Place in a food processor in batches and Pulse until a rice consistency is achieved.

2. Place the cauliflower kernels on paper towels (I use 3 stacked), microwave on high for 3 minutes (I do 2 batches for 1 head of cauliflower.)

3. Place the cauliflower in a dry clean tea towel and squeeze to drain any remaining moisture: This is key!!!

4. In a large bowl mix the cheeses and eggs and salt and garlic powder. Stir in the cauliflower.

5. Press this mixture into the Flip Pan™ on the grill side.

6. Assemble Triple Flip Pan™ by attaching the griddle base to the circle cover and preheat over medium heat for 3–4 minutes per side.

7. Attach the lid to the Flip Pan™ and place grill side down on medium low burner.

8. Cook for 5 minutes. Increase heat to medium and cook for 5 minutes longer.

Corned Beef Hash

Serves 6

INGREDIENTS

1 package (20 ounces) cubed fresh potato cubes (from refrigerator section)

1 pound cooked corned beef, cut into ½ -inch cubes

1 tablespoon extra-virgin olive oil

¼ cup celery, finely chopped

1 small onion, diced

¼ teaspoon freshly ground pepper

½ teaspoon sea salt

2 tablespoons flat leaf parsley, chopped

6 large fresh eggs

DIRECTIONS

1. Assemble Triple Flip Pan™ by attaching the griddle base pan to the grill cover and preheat over medium heat for 3–4 minutes per side.

2. Add oil and when oil is heated add onions and celery. Cook for 4–6 minutes or until just tender.

3. Add potatoes, corned beef and stir, close lid and cook 4 minutes, Flip Pan™ and cook an additional 4 minutes or until golden brown.

4. Open lid, season with salt and pepper. Make 6 wells in the hash, and crack an egg in each well; Close lid.

5. Cook 1 minute or until desired doneness of egg.

6. Open lid and sprinkle with parsley and serve.

Island Fish

Serves 6–8

INGREDIENTS

2 ½ pounds Mahi Mahi, or any firm fish

2 large tomatoes, cut into large chunks

2 large onions, cut into large chunks

6 cloves garlic, chopped

2 tablespoons Worcestershire sauce

1 teaspoon dried thyme

1 teaspoon sea salt

1 teaspoon freshly ground pepper

1 ½ tablespoon extra-virgin olive oil

1 cup seafood stock

DIRECTIONS

1. Assemble Triple Flip Pan™ by attaching the griddle base pan to the grill cover and preheat over medium heat for 3–4 minutes per side.

2. Add oil, heat, add onions and garlic, cook for 1 minute with lid open, add all ingredients except fish; close lid

3. Over medium heat cook for 15 minutes to reduce liquid and cook vegetables, shaking occasionally.

4. Open lid, add fish, close lid and cook for an additional 6–7 minutes or until fish is fully cooked through.

Lemon Butter Chicken with Capers

Serves 6

INGREDIENTS

8 bone-in, skin-on chicken thighs

1 tablespoon smoked paprika

Kosher sea salt and freshly ground pepper to taste

3 tablespoon unsalted, divided

3 cloves garlic, minced

1 cup chicken stock

2 tablespoon capers

½ cup heavy cream

¼ cup Parmesan cheese, grated

2 tablespoons fresh lemon juice

1 teaspoon dried thyme

2 cups baby spinach, chopped

DIRECTIONS

1. Assemble Triple Flip Pan™ by attaching the griddle base pan to the grill cover and preheat over medium heat for 3–4 minutes per side.

2. Add 2 tablespoons butter and heat. Sprinkle chicken with sea salt and pepper on both sides and add to Flip Pan™ skin side down; close lid.

3. Cook for 2–3 minutes, flip the pan and cook for an additional 2–3 minutes.

4. Remove chicken to a pan, and drain excess fat and set chicken aside.

5. Melt remaining butter in Flip Pan™, add garlic and capers and cook with lid open for 1 minute, stirring occasionally for about 1–2 minutes.

6. Add chicken broth, heavy cream, Parmesan, lemon juice and thyme; bring to a boil. Reduce heat and stir in spinach, close lid and let simmer until the spinach is wilted and the sauce has thickened, about 2–3 minutes.

7. Return the chicken to the Flip Pan™, close lid and cook for additional 10 minutes, or an internal temperature of 175 degrees.

8. Serve immediately.

Merlot Mushroom Pork Chops

Serves 4

INGREDIENTS

4 bone-in center cut pork chops

2 tablespoons olive oil

½ cup flour

1 teaspoon sea salt

1 teaspoon garlic powder

½ teaspoon freshly ground pepper

¼ teaspoon sweet paprika

2 cups portabella mushrooms, sliced

2 garlic cloves, minced

8 ounces Merlot

½ cup heavy cream

DIRECTIONS

1. On a large plate, mix together flour, paprika, garlic powder, salt and pepper.

2. Assemble Triple Flip Pan™ by attaching the griddle base pan to the grill cover and preheat over medium heat for 3-4 minutes per side. Add oil, when heated add pork chops.

3. Cook for 2 minutes and flip, cook for 3 minutes longer, flip again.

4. Add mushrooms and garlic, close Flip Pan™ and cook for 3 minutes more. Remove chops to a platter.

5. Deglaze the pan with wine scraping up all the bits at the bottom of the pan.

6. Place pork chops back in the Flip Pan™ close lid and cook over medium for 15-20 minutes.

7. Transfer pork chops and mushroom to a platter, cover and keep warm.

8. Increase heat under Flip Pan™ to medium high. Stir in cream and simmer with lid open until reduced by ¼.

9. Pour sauce over chops and serve.

Parmesan Chicken with Blistered Tomatoes

Serves 2-4

INGREDIENTS

2 chicken breasts, boneless, skinless and pounded thin

2 tablespoons extra-virgin olive oil

1-pint cherry or grape tomatoes

4 green onions, sliced thinly

2 cloves garlic, minced

¼ cup dry white wine

2 cups chicken stock

1 cup dry rotini pasta

¼ teaspoon dried thyme

1 tablespoon unsalted butter

4 tablespoons Parmesan cheese

Sea salt and freshly ground pepper to taste

DIRECTIONS

1. Assemble Triple Flip Pan™ by attaching the griddle base pan to the grill surface and preheat over medium heat for 3-4 minutes per side. Add oil and heat.

2. Season chicken on both sides with salt and pepper, place in pan and close lid.

3. Cook for 2-3 minutes, Flip pan and cook for an additional 2-3 minutes. Remove chicken to a plate and set aside.

4. Place tomatoes in pan, close lid and cook until they start to brown and burst, shaking occasionally.

5. Open lid, add onion, garlic and dried thyme and cook for 30 seconds with the lid up.

6. Deglaze pan with stock and wine, add pasta put the chicken with its juices on top, and close lid.

7. Cook until pasta is al dente about 6-8 minutes, and liquid is absorbed. Remove chicken to a serving platter.

8. Add butter and Parmesan to pasta and mix well.

9. Serve with additional Parmesan on the side if desired.

Orange Upside Down Cake

Serves 8–10

INGREDIENTS

1 navel orange, with rind, sliced thin

½ cup unsalted butter

½ cup packed brown sugar

1 tablespoon maple syrup

1 box orange flavored cake mix

3 large eggs

⅓ cup of oil

1 cup of water

Nonstick spray

DIRECTIONS

1. Place the grill side of Triple Flip Pan™ by itself on medium burner for 3–5 minutes.

2. With a mixer, prepare the cake mix by mixing, eggs water and oil with dry cake mix, 1 minute on low, 2 minutes on high.

3. Place the base of the Triple Flip Pan™ on a medium burner and melt the butter, brown sugar and syrup together.

4. When caramel is smooth top with the orange slices.

5. Pour the cake batter over the oranges.

6. Attach the grill side to the Flip Pan™ carefully, close.

7. Cook cake for 10 minutes over medium low.

8. When cook time is complete check for cake doneness with a toothpick, make sure it comes out clean.

9. Remove from the heat and let cake set for 10 minutes before inverting.

10. Serve warm or cold.

Stuffed Salmon with Spinach En Papillote

Serves 4

◆

INGREDIENTS

2 ounces cream cheese, softened

½ cup crumbled feta

⅓ cup onion, minced

½ cup baby spinach, chopped

4 (6 ounce) 1 ½-inch thick salmon filets

4 (10-inch squares) Parchment paper

12 asparagus spears

½ teaspoon sea salt

¼ teaspoon freshly ground pepper

4 tablespoons pesto

DIRECTIONS

1. In a bowl, combine feta, cream cheese, onion and spinach.

2. Cut a pocket in each filet and stuff with equal amounts of spinach mixture.

3. Lay out squares of parchment on a work surface and place 4 spears of asparagus in one layer in the center of each piece of paper.

4. Top each one with a piece of salmon, and season with salt and pepper.

5. Fold parchment over contents; pleat edge to seal, forming a half-moon.

6. Assemble Triple Flip Pan™ by attaching the griddle base pan to the grill cover and preheat over medium heat for 3–4 minutes per side.

7. Place all 4 salmon pouches in the Flip Pan™ and close the lid.

8. Cook 3–4 minutes per side over medium-high heat

9. Carefully cut each pouch open with scissors, removing each salmon filet to a serving platter, and drizzle with pesto and serve.

Sweet and Sour Pork Chops

Serves 4

◆

INGREDIENTS

4 bone-in pork chops, 1-inch thick

1 tablespoon extra-virgin olive oil

½ teaspoon sea salt

1 cup chicken stock

¼ cup brown sugar

1 teaspoon cider vinegar

1 teaspoon freshly grated ginger

½ teaspoon dry mustard

1 teaspoon dried marjoram

¼ cup orange liqueur

1 teaspoon orange zest

1 sprig fresh thyme

½ teaspoon freshly ground pepper

2 oranges, peeled and sectioned

DIRECTIONS

1. Assemble Triple Flip Pan™ by attaching the griddle base pan to the grill cover and preheat over medium heat for 3–4 minutes per side.

2. Season pork chops with salt and rub with olive oil.

3. Place pork chops into Flip Pan™ and sear for 2 minutes each side.

4. Add chicken stock to deglaze pan, scraping up all the bits from the bottom of the pan.

5. Add remaining ingredients; close lid and cook 30 minutes over medium heat.

6. Serve immediately.

Whoopie Pies

Serves 6

INGREDIENTS

1 box Devil's Food cake mix

3 large eggs

½ cup of oil

1 ¼ cups water

2 cups can vanilla frosting

2 cups of marshmallow fluff

Nonstick spray

DIRECTIONS

1. Using a hand or stand mixer, mix the cake mix, eggs, oil and water for 1 minute on low, 2 minutes on high.

2. Assemble Triple Flip Pan™ by attaching the griddle base to the circle cover.

3. Begin preheating the ring side of the Flip Pan™ for 5 minutes over low, flip and preheat the base for 5 minutes over low. Flip again.

4. Spray the rings on the Flip Pan™ and increase the heat to medium.

5. Scoop ¼ cup of prepared cake batter into each ring.

6. Close Flip Pan™ and cook for 4 minutes on medium low.

7. Check for doneness.

8. When cooked through, remove to a cooling rack and repeat with 4 more.

9. Repeat this process until all the batter is used. Most mixes make 12 Whoopie tops.

10. With a mixer, whip frosting and marshmallow fluff.

11. When Whoopie cakes are cool fill with cream and serve.

12. Feel free to use red velvet or other cake mixes.

Caramel Pecan Rolls

Serves 8–10

INGREDIENTS

2 cans (17.5 ounce size) refrigerated cinnamon buns

1 stick of unsalted butter

¾ cup with brown sugar

¼ cup of maple syrup

3 cups whole pecans

Nonstick spray

DIRECTIONS

1. Place the Proaster lid over medium heat.

2. Add the butter and melt.

3. Stir in the brown sugar and maple syrup, stirring constantly until a smooth caramel is reached.

4. Stir in the pecans.

5. Remove the lid from the stove top.

6. Carefully place the cinnamon buns on the pecan mixture.

7. Place the pan in the center rack in the oven.

8. Bake for 15–18 minutes, or desired brownness is achieved.

9. Remove from oven and let rest for 5 minutes, Invert onto a platter or cutting board.

10. Serve warm!

Corned Beef and Cabbage

Serves 4–6

INGREDIENTS

3 pounds corned beef, trimmed

1 large onion, quartered

2 cups beef stock

1 bottle (12 ounces) beer

½ teaspoon mustard seeds

½ teaspoon whole peppercorns

2 allspice berries

1 bay leaf

3 garlic cloves, minced

6 small onions, peeled

6 small bliss potatoes, halved

12 baby carrots

1 head cabbage, cut into 6 wedges

DIRECTIONS

1. Preheat oven to 350 degrees.

2. Place corned beef and onion in Proaster, add in the stock, beer and seasonings; secure lid.

3. Place the Proaster in the oven for 2 hours.

4. When cooking is complete, and pressure is released naturally, open lid.

5. Place the meat on the Proaster lid and Add remaining ingredients to the Proaster base; secure glass lid.

6. Place Proaster on a medium high burner for 20 minutes.

7. When cook time is complete, scoop out the vegetables and place on the lid with the corn beef, ladle some of the juice over and serve.

Flip Pan™ Herb Bread Stuffing

Serves 10-12

INGREDIENTS

8 tablespoons (1 stick) unsalted butter

1 large onion, diced

4 medium ribs celery, dices

½ teaspoon dried sage

½ teaspoon dried thyme

½ teaspoon dried marjoram

½ cup fresh parsley leaves, minced

½ teaspoon freshly ground pepper

12 cups dried ½-inch cubes of French bread

2 cups chicken stock

3 large eggs, beaten lightly

1 teaspoon sea salt

Foil

Nonstick spray

DIRECTIONS

1. Preheat oven to 350 degrees. Adjust rack to middle position.

2. Preheat Proaster lid on the stove over medium heat for 2-3 minutes, add butter and heat until fully melted.

3. Remove 2 tablespoons of butter and reserve. Add onion and celery to the lid and sauté, stirring occasionally until translucent, about 8 minutes.

4. Stir in sage, thyme, marjoram, parsley and black pepper and cook until just fragrant, about a minute longer.

5. Turn onion mixture into a large bowl and add bread cubes, stock, eggs, and salt; toss to distribute dry and wet ingredients evenly.

6. Turn mixture into the Proaster lid sprayed with nonstick spray, drizzle with the reserved melted butter, cover tightly with foil and bake until fragrant, about 25 minutes.

7. Remove foil and bake until a golden brown crust forms on top, about 15-20 minutes longer. Serve warm.

Holiday Ham

Serves 10–12

INGREDIENTS

1 10–12 pound smoked ham

1 20 ounce can pineapple slices, with the juice reserved

8 maraschino cherries

21 whole cloves

1 cup brown sugar

DIRECTIONS

1. Preheat oven to 250 degrees.

2. Decorate the ham half with pineapple slices by piercing with cloves, three per pineapple slice.

3. Place a maraschino cherry in the center of each pineapple ring and secure with a toothpick.

4. Place ham in the Proaster, secure Proaster lid and place in the center rack in the oven for 30 minutes.

5. When cook time is complete, remove the ham and place large side down on the Proaster lid.

6. Combine the brown sugar with 2 tablespoons of reserved pineapple juice and bring to a boil until all the sugar dissolves.

7. Baste the ham with the glaze and place back in the oven for an additional 30 minutes. Basting with glaze every 10 minutes.

8. Remove the ham and sit it upright. Serve at once.

Herb Roasted Leg of Lamb

Serves 4–6

INGREDIENTS

2–3 pound boneless leg of lamb, trussed

4 garlic cloves, minced

1 tablespoon coarse sea salt

2 tablespoons chopped fresh rosemary

½ teaspoon freshly ground pepper

¼ cup red wine, or beef stock

1 tablespoon extra-virgin olive oil

2 rosemary sprigs

DIRECTIONS

1. Pat lamb dry and score the fat by making shallow cuts all over with the tip of a sharp small knife.

2. Combine the garlic, salt, rosemary and pepper. Rub lamb with oil, press the rosemary mixture into the lamb.

3. Place on the lid of the Proaster and let rest for 30 minutes at room temperature.

4. Preheat oven to 350 degrees. Roast lamb on middle rack until an instant-read thermometer inserted 2-inches into the thickest part of the meat reads 135 degrees, 1 ¼ to 1 ½ hours.

5. Transfer to a cutting board and let rest for 15–20 minutes, (internal temperature will rise to about 140 degrees for medium-rare).

6. Pour off any fat from the pan, add wine or stock to the pan and deglaze by boiling over medium high heat, stirring and scrapping up all the brown bits, about 1 minute.

7. Season pan juices with salt and pepper and serve with lamb.

8. Garnish with rosemary sprigs.

Maple Glazed Pork Loin with Apples and Caramelized Onions

Serves 6-8

INGREDIENTS

3-4 pounds boneless pork loin

2 large sweet onions, sliced thin

2 apples, peeled, cored and quartered

2 tablespoons olive oil

½ teaspoon sea salt

¼ teaspoon freshly ground pepper

¼ teaspoon fennel seeds (optional)

1 tablespoon maple syrup

¼ cup chicken stock

¼ cup apple cider

2 tablespoons butter

DIRECTIONS

1. Preheat oven to 400 degrees.

2. Preheat bottom of the Proaster on the stove over medium heat for 2 minutes. Add oil and heat for 2 minutes.

3. Rub the pork with salt and pepper, place on Proaster and sear on all sides.

4. Add onions and apples and cook until golden brown. Add fennel seeds if using, and drizzle maple syrup over the top of the roast add in the apple cider.

5. Cover Proaster with lid, lock on firmly and place in the oven on the middle rack. Reduce heat 350 degrees.

6. Cook for approximately 15 minutes per pound.

7. When cooking is complete, place the roast on the lid and cover with apples and onions; cover with foil and let rest.

8. Place the Proaster base on the stove over medium heat.

9. Add chicken stock and scape up all the brown bits on the bottom; reduce liquid by half while scraping.

10. Add 1 tablespoon of butter. When dissolved, add the other tablespoon of butter. Heat to form a glaze.

11. Slice the roast and serve on the lid as a platter, drizzle with glaze.

Piña Colada Dump Cake

Serves 16–20

INGREDIENTS

2 cups (4 sticks butter) divided

2/3 cup rum

2 cans (20-ounce size) Pineapple chunks, drained

2 (15.25 oz.) box yellow cake mix

3 cups sweetened flaked coconut

Whipped cream for garnish

DIRECTIONS

1. Preheat oven to 350 degrees.

2. Place the Proaster lid on a medium burner.

3. Place 2 sticks of butter in the lid and let melt.

4. Add the rum and pineapple and cook for 2 minutes.

5. Remove the lid from the stove.

6. Cut the remaining butter into 1 tablespoon size pieces.

7. Sprinkle the two cake mixes over the pineapple mixture evenly.

8. Sprinkle the coconut over the cake mix, top with the pieces of butter evenly places.

9. Place the cake in the center of the oven and bake for 45–60 minutes.

10. Check cake to make sure the coconut is not getting too dark, after 40 minutes.

11. If it is tent with aluminum foil.

12. Cake is fully cooked when a toothpick inserted in the center comes out clean.

13. Serve hot or cold topped with whip cream.

Pork Roast with Apples, Carrots and Rosemary

Serves 6-8

INGREDIENTS

4 pounds pork roast, boneless

4 large carrots, cut in large chunks

2 Granny Smith apples, cored and cut in
  8 wedges each

1 large onion, cut in 8 wedges

1 sprig fresh rosemary

¼ teaspoon dried thyme

1 tablespoon fresh lemon juice

Kosher sea salt and coarsely ground pepper

1 tablespoon extra-virgin olive oil

DIRECTIONS

1. Preheat oven to 350 degrees.

2. In a bowl, combine apples and lemon juice and toss; set aside.

3. Season the roast with salt, pepper, and thyme. Place half the onions and apples in the Proaster, Place the roast on top of them and surround the roast with the carrots, and the rest of the onions and apples.

4. Top with sprig of rosemary and season with salt and pepper.

5. Drizzle with olive oil, close lid and place in oven. Bake for 30 minutes, remove lid and cook for an additional 15 minutes or until the internal temperature on meat thermometer reads 155 degrees.

6. Open lid, remove roast to a platter let rest for 5 minutes, slice and top with apple, onion, and carrots.

Proaster Prime Rib of Beef

Serves 6–8

◆

INGREDIENTS

1 6-pound prime rib roast, bone in

1 tablespoon olive oil

1 tablespoon course sea salt or kosher salt

1 tablespoon fresh cracked pepper

1 teaspoon garlic powder

1 large sweet onion sliced thin

1 sprig thyme

1 sprig rosemary

1 cup beef stock

1 cup port wine

DIRECTIONS

1. Rub the rib roast with oil salt pepper and garlic powder.

2. Wrap tightly with plastic wrap and refrigerate overnight.

3. Set roast out at room temperature for 40 minutes before cooking.

4. Preheat oven to 500 degrees.

5. Place the base of the Proaster on a low burner for 3 minutes.

6. Add the sliced onions to cover the base of Proaster.

7. Top the onions with herbs, place the roast (rib side down) on top of the onions and secure the Proaster lid.

8. Place the Proaster in the center rack in the oven.

9. Reduce the temperature of the oven to 250 degrees.

10. Cook for 2 hours with lid on.

11. Using a meat thermometer check for internal temperature registers 120–135 degrees in the very center of the roast.

12. Remove Proaster from the oven and carefully place the prime rib on the lid of Proaster and tent with aluminum foil.

13. Turn oven to 500 degrees.

14. After 30 minutes of resting, remove the foil and cook the prime rib for 5 minutes until dark and crusty and the internal temperature is 128–130 degrees for perfect medium rare.

15. Remove and let roast rest.

16. Place the Proaster base over medium high heat. Remove the onions and herbs to a cutting board and skim off any fat if you can.

17. Add the wine and the beef stock to the Proaster scraping up the browned bits off the bottom of the pan.

18. Let the liquid cook until reduced by half.

19. Serve as au jus on the side of roast.

Spinach Stuffed Shells

Serves 8

INGREDIENTS

1 12-ounce box jumbo pasta shells

2 teaspoons kosher salt divided

1 pound lean ground beef

1 medium onion minced

3 cloves garlic minced

½ teaspoon pepper

½ teaspoon crushed red pepper flakes

½ teaspoon Italian seasoning

2 28-ounce cans crushed tomatoes

¼ cup fresh basil chopped

1 cup fresh spinach leaves stems removed, chopped

2 cups whole milk ricotta

1 cup shredded Mozzarella

½ cup grated Parmesan cheese

1 large egg, lightly beaten

DIRECTIONS

1. Preheat oven to 350 degrees.

2. Fill Proaster half way with water and place on a burner over medium high heat.

3. Cover with glass lid and bring to a boil. Season water with half the salt.

4. When water comes to a boil add shells and stir. Cover with the lid and let boil for 6 minutes.

5. Strain through a colander; rinse with cold water.

6. Place the Proaster back on the stove and heat on medium high heat.

7. Add the ground beef to the Proaster and cook until browned breaking up with a wooden spoon while cooking about 3–4 minutes.

8. Add the onions and garlic salt and pepper and pepper flakes and cook for another minute.

9. Add the Italian seasoning and the tomatoes and cook over medium low heat stirring occasionally for 20 minutes.

10. In a large mixing bowl combine the basil, spinach, ricotta and ½ cup of mozzarella cheese.

11. Stir in ¼ cup Parmesan cheese and beaten egg.

12. Stuff each cooked shell with mixture.

13. When 20 minutes is complete gently place the shells in the Proaster in the sauce.

14. Sprinkle the top with the remaining mozzarella and Parmesan.

15. Top with the lid place in the oven.

16. Bake for 40 minutes.

17. Sprinkle with fresh parsley and serve.

Scalloped Potatoes Au Gratin

Serves 8–10

INGREDIENTS

8 russet potatoes, peeled and cut into ⅛-inch thick slices

2 sweet onions, sliced thin

½ butter or margarine

1 tablespoon all-purpose flour

1 teaspoon sea salt

½ teaspoon freshly ground pepper

2 cups milk

2 cups (8 ounces) cheddar cheese, shredded

¼ cup Parmesan, shredded

Nonstick spray

DIRECTIONS

1. Preheat oven to 375 degrees. Peel potatoes cut into ⅛ slices place in a large bowl of water to prevent browning and to remove the starch.

2. Preheat Proaster base over medium heat for 2–3 minutes. Add butter and when heated add onion.

3. Cook 2 minutes stirring occasionally until tender. Stir in flour, salt and pepper.

4. Cook stirring constantly until bubbly; remove from heat and stir in milk and cheeses;

5. Return base to the heat and bring to a simmer stirring constantly. Simmer and stir for 2 minutes.

6. Pat potatoes dry with paper towels. Spray Proaster lid with nonstick spray.

7. Spread the potatoes out evenly over the Proaster and pour the cheese mixture over the potatoes.

8. Place lid on the center rack in the oven and bake for 20–25 minutes or until golden brown and bubbly.

9. Serve warm sprinkle with fresh chives.

UniVersa Junior Flip Pan™

Chicken with Yellow Rice

Serves 4–6

INGREDIENTS

1 package (16 ounces) yellow rice mix

4 boneless, skinless chicken breasts, cubed

2 tablespoons extra-virgin olive oil

1 teaspoon sea salt

½ teaspoon freshly ground pepper

5 cups water

1 cup frozen peas

½ cup Spanish olives

DIRECTIONS

1. Add the oil to the Flip Pan™. Heat for 2–3 minutes.

2. Add the chicken to the pan and brown on all sides.

3. Season with salt and pepper.

4. Add the water and stir in the yellow rice mixtures.

5. Close lid and cook for 20 minutes over medium.

6. Stir in the olives and peas.

7. Close lid and cook for 2 minutes longer.

8. When all liquid has evaporated serve hot.

Chicken Stew with Cauliflower and Olives

Serves 4

INGREDIENTS

2 tablespoons extra-virgin olive oil, divided

4 chicken thighs, bone-in

2 tablespoons red wine vinegar

1 large onion, chopped

Sea salt and freshly ground pepper to taste

3 garlic cloves, minced

1 can (28 ounces) petite diced tomatoes

½ teaspoon cinnamon

1 teaspoon fresh thyme leaves

1 small or ½ large head cauliflower, cored, broken into florets and sliced into ½ -inch pieces.

12 Kalamata olives, pitted

2 tablespoons chopped flat leaf parsley

2 ounces feta cheese, crumbled

DIRECTIONS

1. Preheat Flip Pan™ over medium-high heat for 2–3 minutes.

2. Season chicken with salt and pepper on both sides.

3. Add 1 tablespoon oil and heat; Place chicken in Flip Pan™ skin side down, close lid and cook for 5 minutes.

4. Open lid and flip chicken and cook for an additional 5 minutes. Open lid and remove chicken to a plate.

5. Pour off any excess fat and add vinegar to deglaze pan scraping up all the bits from the bottom of the pan.

6. Add the remaining oil to Flip Pan™, reduce heat to medium. Add onion and a good pinch of salt and cook, stirring often, scraping the bottom of the pan.

7. Close lid and cook about 3–4 minutes until onions are soft. Turn heat to low, and cook for an additional 6–8 minutes, stirring occasionally until slightly browned.

8. Open lid, add garlic, stir, and cook with lid open for 1 minute, until garlic is fragrant.

9. Add tomatoes, cinnamon, thyme, salt and pepper to taste. Close lid, bring to a simmer.

10. Cook for 10 minutes stirring occasionally, until liquid is slightly reduced.

11. Open lid and return chicken to Flip Pan™, close lid and simmer for an additional 15–20 minutes.

12. Open lid, add cauliflower and Kalamata olives. Close lid and cook for 10–15 minutes or until cauliflower is tender and chicken is following off the bone.

13. Open lid, sprinkle with parsley and feta; Serve immediately.

Creamy Chicken and Bacon Linguini with Spinach and Tomatoes in a Garlic Sauce

Serves 4–6

INGREDIENTS

6 bacon strips, chopped

1-½ pounds chicken tenders

1 teaspoon paprika

1 teaspoon Italian seasoning

5 medium sized tomatoes, chopped in large cubes

3 cups fresh baby spinach

5 cloves garlic, minced

1 tablespoon crushed red pepper

¼ teaspoon sea salt

¼ teaspoon freshly ground pepper

1 ⅓ cup half and half

1 ½ cups Parmesan cheese, shredded

1 pound linguini, cooked and drained

DIRECTIONS

1. Preheat Flip Pan™ on medium heat for 2–3 minutes.

2. Add chopped bacon, and cook until fat is rendered and crisp. Remove with a slotted spoon and set aside.

3. Season chicken with salt, paprika and Italian seasoning. Add chicken, close lid and cook for 1 minute.

4. Turn the chicken tenders and cook for an additional 3 minutes.

5. Remove chicken to a platter.

6. Add spinach, red pepper and garlic to the pan, cook for 1 minute with the lid open.

7. Add tomatoes, close lid and cook for 2 minutes. Open lid and add chicken, bacon and half and half.

8. When it comes to a boil, add Parmesan cheese. Reduce to a simmer and close lid.

9. Cook, while stirring occasionally, for 1 minute. Remove from heat.

10. Open lid, and stir in pasta and serve.

Curried Spaghetti Squash

Serves 4

◆

INGREDIENTS

1 medium spaghetti squash (2 ½-3lbs)

¼ cup chicken stock

1 tablespoon butter

Teaspoon freshly grated ginger

1 teaspoon garam masala

1 tablespoon lemon juice

1 tablespoon of honey

½ teaspoon of sea salt

2 tablespoons fresh cilantro leaves chopped

DIRECTIONS

1. Cut the squash in half lengthwise and scoop out seeds.

2. Preheat Flip Pan™ over medium heat for 2 minutes.

3. Place the squash halves and chicken stock in the UniVersa Junior Flip Pan™.

4. Close Flip Pan™ lid and raise temperature to medium high. Set timer for 18 minutes.

5. When cook time is complete, remove the squash from the Flip Pan™ to cool, pour any remaining chicken stock over the squash.

6. Add the butter to the Flip Pan™ and over medium let melt, add the ginger and garam masala and cook for 2 minutes.

7. Stir in the lemon juice and honey and salt.

8. Scrape the flesh of the squash in to the Flip Pan™ and toss with butter and spices.

9. Toss in the cilantro and serve at once.

Easy Butter Chicken

Serves 4

---◆---

INGREDIENTS

Spice Blend

1 tablespoon garam masala seasoning

1 ½ teaspoons ground ginger

½ teaspoon ground cinnamon

¼ teaspoon cayenne pepper

1 teaspoon sea salt

1 tablespoon olive oil

2 boneless skinless chicken breasts, or 4 boneless thighs cut into 1 inch chunks

3 tablespoons butter

1 cup of onion diced

4 cloves of garlic minced

1 tablespoon tomato paste

1 15-ounce can tomato sauce

1 14 ½ ounce petite diced tomatoes

⅓ cup heavy whipping cream

Hot basmati rice on the side

Green onions for garnish

DIRECTIONS

1. Blend the ingredients for the spice blend.

2. Rub the chicken pieces well with the spice.

3. Preheat the Flip Pan™ top and bottom over medium heat.

4. Add the oil to the pan and heat for 2 minutes.

5. Add the chicken pieces to the pan, close the lid.

6. Cook the chicken for 3 minutes, flip and cook for 3 minutes longer.

7. Add the butter to the Flip Pan™ over medium heat and just melt.

8. Add the onions to the Flip pan and close the lid and cook for 2 minutes.

9. Add the garlic to the Flip Pan™ and cook 1 minute longer.

10. Add the tomato paste and any remaining spices to the Flip Pan™ and stir the paste to ensure not to burn.

11. Add the tomato sauce and tomatoes close the lid and cook for 5 minutes.

12. Stir in heavy cream.

13. Serve over hot basmati rice garnished with green onions.

Mediterranean Macaroni and Cheese

Serve 4–6

◆

INGREDIENTS

5 plum tomato slices

½ teaspoon dried thyme

¼ teaspoon garlic powder

¼ teaspoon sea salt

1 tablespoon extra-virgin olive oil

3 cups chicken stock

1 box (12 ounces) one pan-no boil-no drain elbow macaroni

2 cup half and half

4 ounces cream cheese, softened

6 ounces sharp cheddar cheese, shredded

3 ounces Fontina cheese, shredded

2 ½ ounces Parmesan cheese, grated

4 ½ ounces (½ package) artichoke hearts, thawed and halved

DIRECTIONS

1. Pour stock into Flip Pan™ and add elbows; close lid and until liquid has evaporated, about 10 minutes.

2. Meanwhile, turn the oven on to broil and place tomato slices on a baking sheet and drizzle with oil. Sprinkle with thyme, garlic powder, and sea salt.

3. Place baking sheet under the broiler for 8–10 minutes, or until lightly browned. Transfer to a plate and set aside.

4. When elbows are cooked, open lid and stir in cream cheese and half and half until cream cheese is dissolved, stir in cheddar cheese, Fontina cheese and Parmesan. Gently stir in artichoke hearts.

5. Top with tomato slices and serve.

Pasta with Red Clam Sauce

Serves 4

◆

INGREDIENTS

1 teaspoon kosher sea salt

1 pound linguine, cooked al dente

2 tablespoons extra-virgin olive oil

1 can (2 ounces) anchovy filets, drained

½ teaspoon red pepper flakes

½ teaspoon dried thyme

¼ teaspoons dried oregano

4 cloves garlic cloves, minced

1 medium onion, finely chopped

½ cup dry red wine

2 (14 ounces) cans chopped clams, reserve juice

1 (28 ounces) can crushed tomatoes

Sea salt and freshly ground pepper to taste

¼ cup chopped flat leaf parsley

2 tablespoons fresh lemon juice

DIRECTIONS

1. Preheat Flip Pan™ with lid closed for 2 minutes.

2. Add oil, and heat add anchovies close lid and cook until anchovy's melt into the oil. (About a minute)

3. Add red pepper flake, thyme, oregano, and garlic, close lid and cook for 1 minute.

4. Open lid add onion, close lid and cook for 2–3 minutes over medium heat.

5. Open lid, add wine and cook for 1 minute with lid open, add in the lemon juice, clams, and half their juice.

6. Close lid and cook for 1 minute, open lid and add tomatoes, close lid and cook for 5 minutes.

7. Add linguine and toss well with sauce. Close lid for 1 minute with no heat.

8. Season to taste, garnish with parsley.

Shrimp Curry

Serves 4

INGREDIENTS

2 pounds jumbo shrimp, peeled and de-veined

1 cup chicken stock

¼ cup brown sugar

1 tablespoon curry powder

1 teaspoon garam masala

1 medium onion, chopped

1 red bell pepper, julienned

1 can (14 ½ ounces) petite diced tomatoes

1 cup plain yogurt

1 tablespoon fresh cilantro leaves, chopped

DIRECTIONS

1. Preheat Flip Pan™ over medium heat for 2-3 minutes.

2. Place all ingredients except yogurt into Flip Pan™ and close lid.

3. Cook 10 minutes on medium heat; open lid.

4. Transfer shrimp to a platter.

5. Add yogurt to Flip Pan™ and stir.

6. Pour mixture over shrimp and serve.

Seafood Arrabiata

Serves 4

———◆———

INGREDIENTS

8 ounces uncooked fettuccine or pappardelle Pasta

2 tablespoons extra-virgin olive oil, divided

8 ounces scallops, patted dry

8 ounces medium shrimp, peeled, de-veined and patted dry

8 small clams in the shells scrubbed

8 mussels, scrubbed and de-bearded

1 small onion, chopped

½ teaspoon crushed red pepper flakes

4 cloves garlic, minced

2 tablespoon tomato paste

1 (14 ½ ounces) can fire roasted tomatoes

1 (8 ounce) bottle clam juice

2 tablespoons chopped parsley

1 tablespoon thinly sliced fresh basil

DIRECTIONS

1. Cook pasta and drain.

2. Preheat UniVersa Junior Flip Pan™ over medium heat for 2–3 minutes.

3. Add 1 tablespoon oil, heat and add scallops and shrimp, cook for 2–3 minutes, shaking in-between.

4. Remove scallop and shrimp mixture and set side to keep warm. Add remaining oil, and heat.

5. Add onion, red pepper and garlic, close lid and let cook for 1 minute. Open lid and add tomatoes and tomato paste, stir and close lid.

6. Cook for 2 minutes, open lid and add clam juice. Close lid and cook for an additional 2 minutes.

7. Open lid, add clams and mussels, cook for 3 minutes, until clams and mussels open. Discard any unopened shells. Stir in scallop and shrimp and pasta, toss well. Close lid and cook for 1 minutes.

8. Close lid and cook for 1 additional minute. Garnish with parsley and fresh basil and serve.

Thai Spicy Shrimp

Serves 4–6

INGREDIENTS

2 pounds large shrimp, peeled and de-veined

1 can (14 ½) ounces coconut milk

2 teaspoons red curry paste

¼ cup fish sauce

¼ cup chili sauce

2 tablespoons soy sauce

3 tablespoons hot sesame oil

¼ teaspoon lemon zest

½ cup cilantro, chopped

1 cup green onions, chopped

DIRECTIONS

1. In a bowl, combine curry paste, fish sauce, lemon zest, and chili sauce; add shrimp and toss to coat.

2. Pre-heat oil in Flip Pan™ for 2 minutes, add shrimp mixture and close for 2 minutes shaking pan occasionally.

3. Add green onions, close and cook for another 3 minutes. Open lid, add soy sauce and coconut milk; close lid and let simmer for 1–2 minutes

4. Sprinkle with cilantro and serve.

Tex-Mex Noodle Bowl

Serves 6-8

INGREDIENTS

1 ½ pound top round or flank steak, trimmed and thinly sliced into strips

1 teaspoon cumin

¼ teaspoon sea salt

⅛ teaspoon red pepper flakes

2 tablespoons extra-virgin olive oil

2 cloves garlic, minced

3 cans (14 ½ ounces) low sodium beef stock

4 ounces dry angel hair pasta, broken in half

1 red bell pepper, coarsely cut

8 green onions, sliced thinly on the bias

½ cup medium hot salsa

4 tablespoons fresh cilantro, chopped

DIRECTIONS

1. Preheat Flip Pan™ over medium heat for 2-3 minutes.

2. Season meat with salt, and cumin.

3. Add oil to Flip Pan™ and when heated add garlic, cook for about 20 seconds.

4. Add meat, half at a time and cook with lid open for about 2-3 minutes, stirring constantly until slightly pink in the center.

5. Add stock, bring to a boil and add remaining ingredients except green onion and cilantro.

6. Close lid and cook for 4-5 minutes, or until pasta is tender, stirring occasionally.

7. Top with cilantro and green onions and serve.

Classic Cheese Sauce

Serves 4–6

INGREDIENTS

12 ounces heavy cream

¼ teaspoon Dijon mustard

1 pound mild yellow cheddar

DIRECTIONS

1. Preheat Sauce Flip Pan™ over medium heat and add cream, bring to a simmer over high heat.

2. Reduce heat and add mustard and cheese. Gently stir until well mixed.

Easy Lemon Pound Cake

Serves 12

INGREDIENTS

1 Box Lemon Supreme Cake Mix

1 lemon flavor instant pudding 3.4-ounce size

4 large eggs

1 cup of water

⅓ cup of oil

1 container vanilla frosting

1 teaspoon lemon extract

Lemon slices for garnish

Nonstick spray

DIRECTIONS

1. Using a hand or stand mixer, mix, cake mix, pudding mix, eggs, water and oil. Mix for 1 minute on low, 3 minutes on high.

2. Preheat Sauce Flip Pan™ over low heat for 5 minutes per side, spray base with nonstick spray.

3. Scrape the batter into the pan.

4. Bake for 45 minutes or until a toothpick inserted comes out clean.

5. When cook time is complete, remove pan from heat.

6. Let it rest for 15 minutes before inverting onto a cake stand.

7. Place half the frosting in a microwave safe bowl and microwave for 25 seconds.

8. Stir in the lemon extract.

9. Pour glaze over the cake.

10. Garnish with lemon slices.

Farro Pilaf

Serves 4–6

INGREDIENTS

1 tablespoon extra virgin olive oil

1 small onion, sliced

1 cup mushrooms, sliced

2 cloves garlic, minced

1 cup farro

2 ½ cups vegetable stock

¼ teaspoon sea salt

¼ teaspoon freshly ground pepper

DIRECTIONS

1. Preheat Sauce Flip Pan™ on medium heat for 2–3 minutes per side.

2. Add oil and heat; when oil is heated add onions, mushrooms and garlic.

3. Sauté for 5 minutes, add farro and cook for an additional minute.

4. Add stock, salt and pepper; close lid and cook for 20 minutes.

5. Open lid and stir to fluff; serve immediately.

Irish Oatmeal

Serves 2

INGREDIENTS

⅓ cup Irish oatmeal (steel cut oats)

1 cup water

⅛ teaspoon sea salt

½ teaspoon cinnamon

¼ cup brown sugar

1 teaspoon chia seeds

¼ cup blueberries, fresh or frozen

DIRECTIONS

1. Add water to Sauce Flip Pan™, close lid and bring to a boil.

2. Add salt and oats, close lid, reduce to a simmer, and cook for 25 minutes with lid closed.

3. Open Sauce Flip Pan™ and stirring occasionally.

4. Open lid, add cinnamon, brown sugar, chia seeds and blueberries; stir and serve hot.

Italian Risotto

Serves 4

◆

INGREDIENTS

2 tablespoons extra-virgin olive oil

1 large onion, minced

2 garlic cloves, minced

1 cup Arborio rice

3 cups chicken stock

¾ cup Parmesan cheese, grated

DIRECTIONS

1. Preheat Flip Pan™ over medium heat for 2–3 minutes, add oil and heat oil.

2. Add onion and cook for 2 minutes, add garlic and cook another minute

3. Add broth, bring to a boil and add rice; close lid.

4. Occasionally open lid and stir.

5. Cook for 15 minutes.

6. Stir in the cheese.

7. Cook with lid closed for 5 minutes longer.

8. When cook time is complete, open lid, transfer rice to a serving bowl and fluff with a fork.

Italian Brunch Torte

Serves 6–8

INGREDIENTS

2 tubes (8 ounce) refrigerated crescent rolls, divided

Oil for spraying

6 ounces fresh baby spinach

1 cup sliced fresh mushrooms

7 large eggs

1 cup Parmesan, grated

2 teaspoon Italian seasoning

⅛ teaspoon freshly ground pepper

½ pound thinly sliced deli ham

½ pound thinly sliced Genoa salami

½ pound sliced cheddar cheese

2 jars (12 ounces) roasted red peppers, drained, sliced and patted dry

DIRECTIONS

1. Preheat oven to 350 degrees. Using griddle side of pan as a mold for size, take 5 triangles and mold into a crust to the bottom of the pan.

2. Place on a parchment lined baking sheet, and repeat with remaining triangles to make 3 crusts total.

3. Bake for 10–15 minutes or until set.

4. Meanwhile, preheat Flip Pan™ on each side over medium heat for 2–3 minutes.

5. Spray inside Flip Pan™ on both sides, and add spinach and mushrooms; close lid and cook until mushrooms are tender. Drain on paper towels, blotting well.

6. In a large bowl, whisk eggs, Parmesan cheese, pepper and Italian seasoning.

7. Place one crust in Flip Pan™ and layer with ham, salami, cheddar, red peppers, and the spinach mixture.

8. Pour half the egg mixture over the top. Place another crust on top and repeat the layer, followed by the other half of the egg mixture and the final crust on top.

9. Reduce oven temperature to 300 degrees, and put torte in the over with the lid off for 10 minutes; turn oven off and leave torte in the oven for an additional 10 minutes.

10. Attach Flip Pan™ lid and invert pan, slide torte onto platter and serve.

Mashed Potatoes

Serves 4–6

INGREDIENTS

2 pounds Yukon gold potatoes, peeled and quartered

1 teaspoon sea salt

½ teaspoon fresh ground pepper

Pinch nutmeg (optional)

1 cup chicken stock

½ cup milk or half and half

2 ounces butter

DIRECTIONS

1. Place potatoes, salt, and chicken stock into Flip Pan™, close lid and cook for 25 minutes. Warm butter and milk.

2. When cook time is complete check for tenderness, strain potatoes and place in a bowl.

3. Mash with a potato masher or put through a ricer, add milk and butter and stir.

4. Sprinkle with pepper and serve immediately.

Mediterranean Parsnips

Serves 6–8

INGREDIENTS

3 ½ pound parsnips, peeled and sliced into ¼-inch thick slices

1 cup chicken stock

Sprig thyme

¼ teaspoon kosher sea salt

¼ teaspoon freshly ground pepper

1 cup Kalamata olives, pitted and coarsely chopped

½ cup (3 ½ ounce) capers, drained

DIRECTIONS

1. Add the chicken stock, parsnips and thyme sprig to Flip Pan™, add the pepper and salt.

2. Close lid and cook for 10 minutes or until tender.

3. Drain parsnips, place in a bowl and gently toss with olives, salt, pepper and capers.

4. Serve immediately.

Perfect Grits

Serves 4–6

INGREDIENTS

2 teaspoons kosher sea salt

1 quart water

1 cup stone ground grits

2 tablespoons half and half

2 ½ tablespoons butter

DIRECTIONS

1. Bring water to boil in sauce Flip Pan™ over high heat.

2. Whisk in grits and cook whisking constantly 45 seconds. Return to a boil and reduce heat to medium-low. Add in the salt with the grits (whisk in grits and salt).

3. Close lid and cook for 20–25 minutes or until tender. Open lid and stir in half and half and butter until butter is melted, and serve.

Simple Quinoa

Serves 4

INGREDIENTS

1 cup quinoa

2 cups chicken broth or water

DIRECTIONS

1. Wash quinoa in a fine mesh strainer under cool water. Drain well.

2. Place the Sauce Flip Pan™ on medium high heat, add chicken broth or water, cover and bring liquid to a boil.

3. Stir in quinoa.

4. Reduce heat to low, and close lid, and let simmer for 20 minutes.

5. Remove pan from heat and keep lid closed for another 5–10 minutes. Remove quinoa to a boil and fluff with a fork.

Perfect White Rice

Serves 6

INGREDIENTS

3 cups Long grain rice rinsed well, drained

4 ½ cups water

Pinch of salt

DIRECTIONS

1. Place the Sauce Flip Pan™ over medium high heat filled with the water.

2. Bring the water to a boil with lid closed.

3. Stir in the rice and salt.

4. When the liquid returns to a boil, close the Flip Pan™ lid and reduce the heat to medium.

5. Set a timer for 15 minutes.

6. When cook time is complete remove the rice from the stove and let set for 5 minutes longer before fluffing.

Sriracha Fried Rice

Serves 4-6

INGREDIENTS

½ teaspoons fresh ginger, minced

1 clove garlic, minced

5-6 fresh shitake mushrooms, stems removed, finely chopped

½ cup bean sprouts

3 scallions, white and green parts separated and sliced finely

3 cups cooked rice, cold

1 large egg, beaten

3 tablespoons Sriracha

3 tablespoons soy sauce

2 tablespoons sesame oil

Salt and pepper to taste

DIRECTIONS

1. Preheat Flip Pan™ over medium heat, add oil and heat for 1 minute.

2. Add cold rice breaking up while browning with lid open for 3 minutes.

3. Add remaining ingredients, except egg.

4. Close lid and cook over medium heat 4 minutes.

5. Open lid and stir in egg, close lid and cook for additional 1 minute.

6. Open lid; stir in scallions and serve.

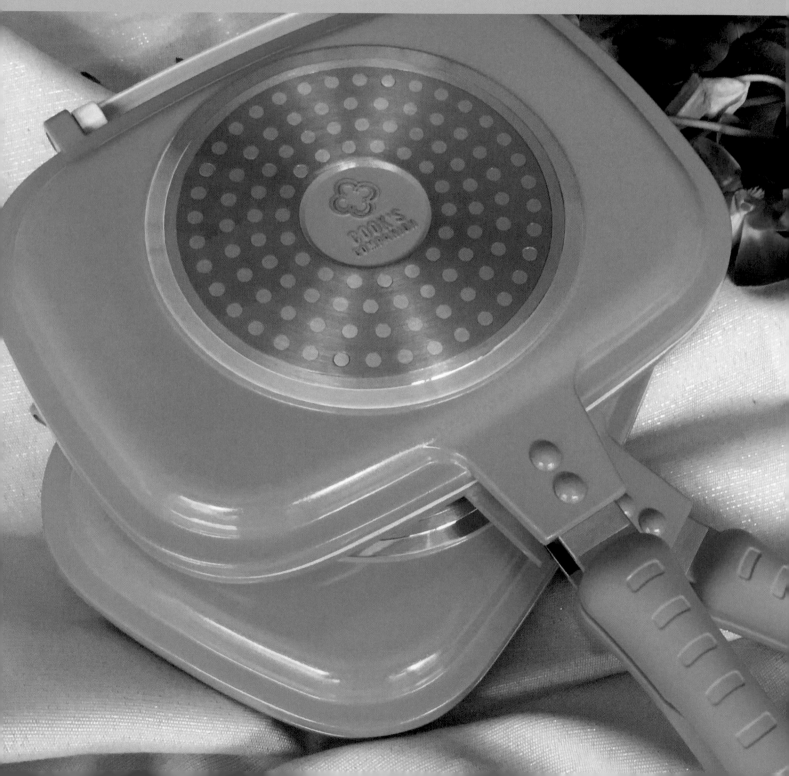

Avocado Caprese Chicken

Serves 4

INGREDIENTS

2 boneless chicken breasts

½ teaspoon garlic powder

½ teaspoon onion powder

½ teaspoon Italian seasoning

¼ teaspoon sea salt

¼ teaspoon freshly ground pepper

2 tablespoons extra-virgin olive oil

6 ounces fresh mozzarella, cut into 8 slices

4 avocado slices, firm and ripe

2 medium heirloom tomatoes, sliced

3 tablespoons balsamic glaze

⅓ cup chopped basil ribbons

DIRECTIONS

1. In a bowl, mix together garlic powder, onion, Italian seasoning, sea salt and pepper. Season chicken on both sides with season mixture.

2. Preheat Flip Pan™ on each side over medium heat for 2–3 minutes per side.

3. Add oil and heat; add chicken, close lid, cook 2–3 minutes, Flip pan and continue to cook for another 2–3 additional minutes or until golden brown on each side.

4. Top each breast with 2 slices of mozzarella, followed by 1 avocado slice and 2 slices of tomato; close lid.

5. Cook 2–3 minutes, open lid and drizzle with balsamic glaze, sprinkle with basil and serve.

Bananas Foster

Serves 1–2

INGREDIENTS

2 ripe bananas, peeled, cut lengthwise

2 tablespoons unsalted butter

½ cup packed brown sugar

1 tablespoon maple syrup

¼ teaspoon cinnamon

2 tablespoon Banana liquor

¼ cup dark rum

Vanilla ice cream to serve on

DIRECTIONS

1. Place the Easy Flip Pan™ on a medium burner, add the butter and melt.

2. Stir in the brown sugar, cinnamon and maple syrup shaking Flip Pan™ stir until it forms a caramel.

3. Add the bananas and banana liquor to the Flip Pan™. Close the Flip Pan™ and cook for 1 minute.

4. Flip the pan and cook 1 minute longer.

5. Open the Flip Pan™ and add the dark rum.

6. Carefully ignite the rum, gently shaking the pan back in forth basting the bananas until the flame dies.

7. Serve the bananas and sauce over vanilla ice cream.

Grilled Gruyere and Smoked Salmon

Serves 2

INGREDIENTS

4 ounces smoked salmon

4 slices marble rye

2 tablespoons olive oil mayonnaise

1 cup Gruyere cheese, grated

1 teaspoons fresh dill, chopped

½ teaspoon lemon zest

DIRECTIONS

1. Lay out 2 slices of bread on a surface and put ¼ of the cheese, ½ teaspoon fresh dill, ¼ teaspoon lemon zest, followed by 2 ounces of salmon, another ¼ cheese on both slices of bread.

2. Place the other 2 slices of bread on top. Spread a thin layer of mayonnaise on the out sides of the 2 sandwiches,

3. Preheat Flip Pan™ on each side over medium heat. Add the 2 sandwiches and cook for 3 minutes. Flip pan and cook an additional 3 minutes.

4. Serve immediately.

Inside Out Grilled Cheese Sandwich

Serves 2

INGREDIENTS

4 slices Brioche Bread

4 teaspoons mayonnaise

½ cup Parmigiano-Reggiano fresh grated

4 slices sharp cheddar cheese

4 slices Swiss cheese

DIRECTIONS

1. Preheat Easy Flip Pan™ top and bottom over medium heat for 3 minutes per side.

2. Spread a teaspoon of mayonnaise on each slice of bread, press into the Parmigiano.

3. Assemble each sandwich with grated cheese side down alternate cheddar and Swiss for each sandwich.

4. Place the sandwiches in the Flip Pan™ and cook for 4 minutes, flip and cook 3 minutes longer or until desired color is achieved.

5. Remove and let cool before cutting.

Italian Cabbage

Serves 4–6

INGREDIENTS

2 cups cabbage, shredded

1 pound hot Italian sausage, sliced in 1-inch cubes

1 small onion, sliced

2 cloves garlic, minced

1 can (14 ½ ounces) diced tomatoes

½ cup chicken stock

½ teaspoon sea salt

¼ teaspoon freshly ground pepper

DIRECTIONS

1. Preheat Flip Pan™ on each side over medium heat for 2–3 minutes per side.

2. Place sausage in Flip Pan™, close lid and cook for 5 minutes, Flip pan and cook for an additional 5 minutes.

3. Pour off excess fat add onion and garlic and cook while stirring for 1 minute.

4. Add tomatoes, cabbage, stock, salt and pepper; close lid and cook over medium heat for 10 minutes.

5. Serve immediately.

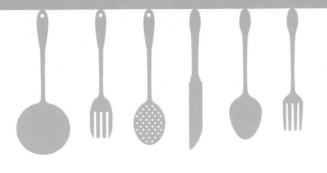

Ratatouille

Serves 4–6

INGREDIENTS

2 tablespoons extra-virgin olive oil

1 small eggplant, diced

1 zucchini, diced

1 yellow squash, diced

1 red bell pepper, diced

2 cloves garlic, minced

1 can (14 ½ ounces) petite diced tomatoes

½ teaspoon fresh thyme, chopped

Sea salt and freshly ground pepper to taste

DIRECTIONS

1. Preheat Flip Pan™ on each side over medium heat 2–3 minutes per side.

2. Add oil and heat; add remaining ingredients, close lid and cook for 5–6 minutes, shaking occasionally.

3. Flip pan, and continue to cook while shaking occasionally for 5–6 additional minutes.

4. Serve warm.

Korean Style Salmon

Serves 2

INGREDIENTS

2 salmon filets 1 ½ inch thick

4 cloves garlic minced

1 teaspoon fresh grated ginger

2 tablespoon honey

¼ cup soy sauce, low sodium

2 teaspoon Sriracha

¼ teaspoon red pepper flakes

1 tablespoon olive oil

1 teaspoon sesame oil

DIRECTIONS

1. In a bowl whisk together the soy sauce, honey, garlic, ginger, red pepper flakes, sesame oil and Sriracha. Pour over the salmon filets and marinade for 20 minutes.

2. Preheat Flip Pan™ on each side over medium heat for 2–3 minutes per side.

3. Add oil and heat for 2 minutes. Add salmon to Flip Pan™, without the marinade and close lid.

4. Cook for 2 minutes, flip the pan and cook for another 2 minutes.

5. Open lid and add marinade, cook with lid open for 1–2 minutes, being careful not to over-cook.

Lemon Garlic Asparagus

Serves 2–4

INGREDIENTS

1 pound asparagus, trimmed

3 tablespoons Parmesan cheese, grated

1 lemon, juice and 1 teaspoon zest

½ teaspoon Sea salt

½ teaspoon freshly ground pepper

DIRECTIONS

1. Preheat Flip Pan™ on each side over medium heat for 2–3 minutes per side.

2. Add asparagus, salt, pepper and lemon juice, close lid and cook for 5 minutes, shaking occasionally.

3. Sprinkle with Parmesan and lemon zest, serve warm.

Mediterranean Grilled Cheese

Serves 2

INGREDIENTS

4 slices of white bread

4 slices beefsteak tomatoes

4 ounces Greek feta cheese

4 thin slices red onion

2 cups baby spinach

2 tablespoons Kalamata olives, pitted and sliced

¼ teaspoon sea salt

¼ teaspoon freshly ground pepper

2 tablespoon olive oil mayonnaise

¼ teaspoons dried oregano

DIRECTIONS

1. Lay out 2 slices of bread on a flat surface, sprinkle ¼ of the feta on each slice of bread.

2. Place 2 slices of tomato and 2 slices of onion on each. Sprinkle tomatoes with salt pepper and oregano.

3. Place half the olive slices on each sandwich, then half the spinach on each one, follow by the rest of the feta.

4. Top each with the other slice of bread, and spread a fine layer of the mayonnaise on each side of each sandwich.

5. Preheat the Flip Pan™ on each side over medium heat for 2–3 minutes each side. Place the sandwiches in the Flip Pan™ and close the lid.

6. Cook for 3 minutes, Flip pan and cook for an additional 3 minutes or until golden brown outside gooey inside.

7. Serve immediately.

Reese Stevenson's Bourbon Brown Sugar Pork Chops

Serves 2

INGREDIENTS

2 large pork chops

1 ½ teaspoons brown sugar

1 ½ teaspoons Bourbon seasoning

2 teaspoons apple cider vinegar

¼ cup olive oil

2 tablespoons water

DIRECTIONS

1. Put all ingredients in zip lock bag and make sure the chops are fully coated with marinade.

2. Marinate for at least 1 hour or overnight.

3. Heat Flip Pan™ med/high heat top and bottom for 3 minutes per side.

4. Remove the pork chops from the marinade, reserving the rest of the marinade.

5. Place the pork chops in the pan and with the lid open sear for 2 minutes per side.

6. Lower heat (low/med) and add remaining marinade and cook for 5 minutes, flip and cook for 5 minutes longer.

Sweet and Savory Pork Chops

Serves 2

INGREDIENTS

2 thin pork chops, center cut bone-in

1 tablespoon extra-virgin olive oil

¼ cup brown sugar

4 tablespoon Worcestershire sauce

1 medium sweet onion, thinly sliced

¼ teaspoon sea salt

¼ teaspoon freshly ground pepper

DIRECTIONS

1. Preheat Flip Pan™ over medium heat for 2–3 minutes per side.

2. Add oil and heat over medium heat for 2 minutes.

3. Season pork chops with salt and pepper and add to the Flip Pan™ and close lid.

4. Cook for 3 minutes, Flip pan and cook an additional 3 minutes.

5. Open lid and add remaining ingredients; close lid and cook for 3 minutes.

6. Serve immediately.

Deb's Favorite Sauces and More

Deb's Favorite Pesto

Serves: 8

◆

INGREDIENTS

....

2 garlic cloves

3 tablespoons butter

½ teaspoon freshly ground pepper

½ cup Parmigiano-Reggiano cheese, grated

3 cups fresh basil leaves

1 cup baby spinach leaves

½ cup extra-virgin olive oil

DIRECTIONS

....

1. In a food processor or blender, combine all ingredients, except oil.

2. While processing, slowly drizzle oil into processor.

Index

Notes

Notes